Knots & Stitches

Caitlin Press Inc.
3375 Ponderosa Way
Qualicum Beach, BC V9K 2J8
www.caitlinpress.com

Text and cover design by Vici Johnstone
Cover image by Linda Gibbs
Edited by Catherine Edwards
Printed in Canada

Caitlin Press Inc. acknowledges financial support from the Government
of Canada and the Canada Council for the Arts, and the Province of
British Columbia through the British Columbia Arts Council and the
Book Publisher's Tax Credit.

Library and Archives Canada Cataloguing in Publication
Knots and stitches : community quilts across the harbour / Kristin Miller.
Miller, Kristin, 1946- author.
Canadiana 20230237460 | ISBN 9781773861203 (softcover)
LCSH: Miller, Kristin, 1946- | LCSH: Quilting-British Columbia,
Northern. | LCSH: Community arts projects-British Columbia, North-
ern. | LCSH: Quiltmakers-Canada-Biography. | LCGFT: Autobiogra-
phies.
LCC TT835 .M55 2023 | DDC 746.4609711/1-dc23

Opposite: The tiny settlements of Dodge Cove, Crippen Cove and Salt Lakes are across
the harbour from the city of Prince Rupert, over 1,000 kilometres north of Vancouver, BC.
Map drawn by Iain Lawrence.

Knots & Stitches

COMMUNITY QUILTS ACROSS THE HARBOUR

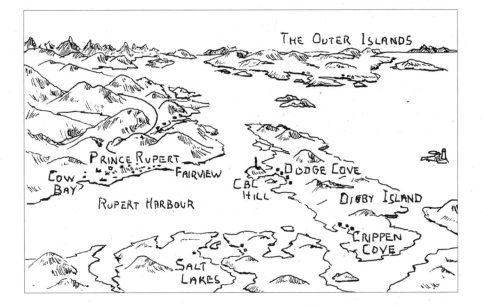

KRISTIN MILLER

Caitlin Press

Opposite: The warmth, colour and communal creativity of our informal quilting circle is celebrated in a painting by Cheryl Hutcheson.

For the quilters,
sisters of my heart.

Contents

Coastal Hopefuls—9

Dreams Go Awry—13

Salt Lakes—18

The Mystery of Life—22

Wild Parties—26

Exceedingly Cautious—29

Stress Test—33

Saltwater Baby Quilts—38

Love and Fishes—46

Salt Lakes Forlorn—56

The Strong Women of Crippen Cove—62

Coming in from the Wilderness Islands—69

Looking for Kids—73

Quilts of Sunshine and Shadow—79

Smitten—87

CBC Hill and Dodge Cove—94

The Quilting Amoebae—102

Hanging Our Quilts on Gallery Walls—109

Visiting Vancouver—115

We Gather Together—121

Living By the Tides—128

Older Now—136

It's Not the End of the Story—144

Acknowledgements—152

Quilt Gallery—153

The Coastal Quilters, 1979 to 2022—161

List of Quilts Mentioned and Additional Links—166

About the Author—168

When I came north in the late seventies, I had no idea how soon, and how drastically, my life would change.

Coastal Hopefuls

The coastal community in the seventies and early eighties was fluid and transient. Prairie kids and city kids and unrepentant hippies fetched up on the docks of Prince Rupert in northern British Columbia looking for the romance of the sea, seeking mystical enlightenment or big bucks in the herring fisheries. A wave of restless adventurers drifted up the coast, coming as far north as they could without bumping into Alaska, as far west as possible without falling into the Pacific. Donning rain gear and sou'westers, they quickly transformed themselves into salty sea dogs. I came north for a short visit in 1977, left, came back, and stayed for twenty-two years.

The coastal hopefuls who moved to Salt Lakes, to Crippen Cove or Dodge Cove, or to the islands beyond the harbour honed their nautical skills with fanatical fervour, learning knots and splices, studying the currents and the tides, gaining the seafaring know-how they needed to survive in this harsh, chilly, water-based world. Most were quick learners, and if they were scared stiff, they didn't show it.

I got my first glimpse of north coast nautical life in 1977 at Function Junction, on the Prince Rupert waterfront—a dilapidated tugboat base

Function Junction was a gathering place, and often a refuge in a storm, for folks coming to town from across the harbour and beyond.

Linda listens as Sébastien and Jane G. perform. Work parties, potlucks and impromptu concerts took place on the wooden deck at Function Junction.

taken over by sea-struck hippies. After a potluck supper and an evening of beer and music, a fierce storm swept up the harbour and everyone rushed outside in the dark of night to make sure their boats were safe. I watched through the rain-streaked window, aghast and admiring as they balanced precariously on the heaving wave-slapped dock and retied their lines. They seemed so stalwart and brave. So foolhardy.

The tiny settlement of Salt Lakes was not on a lake at all. It was a huddle of wind-bleached shanties on the shore of an inlet across the harbour from the town of Prince Rupert. The brackish lake was farther inland, connected to the outer cove by a slough that fed it salt water at the very highest tides. You needed a boat to reach the raggle-taggle community of free spirits living in the cabins and shacks that tilted and swayed on a rocky, windy shore.

An oddball bunch of folks lived at Salt Lakes—hippies and hermits, cannery workers, longshoremen, barmaids, biologists, and fishermen. The women who fished were called fishermen too. The women at Salt Lakes ran their own skiffs and took pride in their chainsaws and in their home-baked bread.

Anyone who wasn't wearing homespun ponchos or gauzy paisley skirts wore the traditional garb of north coast fishermen: scratchy wool Bamberton trousers over slit-seated long johns, red and black plaid shirts with grey wool

Stanfields on top, plus raincoats, rain pants, and gumboots, of course. Residents brewed beer in plastic buckets stashed behind their wood stoves, cooked salmon on the beach, and went clam-digging once or twice before they learned about paralytic shellfish poisoning and the raw sewage that emptied into the Prince Rupert harbour.

In 1979, my boyfriend Bill and I hitched a ride to Salt Lakes on a fishboat, arriving awkwardly at the dock with two over-excited and wildly barking dogs, their leash-

Our tiny cabin is to the right of the large boatshed on the far shore, across from the dock at Salt Lakes.

es tangled in the rigging. We were as excited as the dogs, hiking to the lake along a trail jewelled with red huckleberries. It wound through damp groves of young alder and past a swampy marsh, emerging into sunlight at pink-tinged muskeg meadows where the tops of bonsai'd trees scratched our knees. A broken, sway-backed boardwalk skirted the slough, then continued through salmonberry bushes and deep moss to the lake.

Tangled groups of browning bodies lazed as naked as seal pups on the grass and on the splintery platform in the middle of the lake. I was shocked by all this flesh, but tried not to show it. As we visited Salt Lakes more often, I got used to swimming nude, welcoming the rare rays of sunlight on my skin and the silky feel of the cool water.

We were lucky to buy a sturdy, round-bottomed skiff from Ember at Crippen Cove. He had found the fibreglass shell of a Davidson lifeboat abandoned on the beach and had been able to squeeze the sides together and carry the narrowed boat carcass through the door of his cabin. He completely restored it with oak gunwales and runners, applewood knees, and a mahogany transom. He recreated a broad, beautiful skiff, but of course it no longer fit through the doorway. So he cut away the back wall of his cabin to launch it. We gave him $800 and a handmade quilt in exchange for a boat that safely handled many a storm.

We bought a run-down cabin on the inlet at Salt Lakes for $3,500 but we didn't own the land it sat on, though it only cost $70 a year to lease

a vaguely defined plot of land. We kept our tiny apartment in Rupert and played house at Salt Lakes, spending romantic candlelit evenings at the cabin, then going back to our real life in town. We imagined settling down in this slipshod paradise, but as it turned out, I ended up living there alone.

I was a nervous boater and felt very grateful for the strength and stability of our fourteen-foot Davidson skiff.

Dreams Go Awry

"Because of love," is what I'd sometimes answer when asked why I had moved to Prince Rupert. But the answer was really more complicated. Bill and I were landed immigrants who had moved to Vancouver Island from Seattle in 1974 when I found work there as an occupational therapist. I was a weekend hippie, wearing a uniform and working at the hospital during the week and making quilts to sell at craft fairs on the weekend. Living in a tranquil pastoral setting fulfilled some of my romantic dreams of a rose-covered cottage and a white picket fence.

But Bill's ideas of romance were different. He was drawn by the romance of the north, the wilderness, the sea, and would be gone for months at a time, building roads or deckhanding on fishing boats up north while I stayed alone. He'd come back south for a while, then he'd be gone again. Finally, it seemed that I was always waiting for him to return, so in 1978, I decided to move to Prince Rupert to be with him.

We rented a two-room apartment, and Bill was home from work every night. I set my sewing machine up in a tiny nook in the hallway and made improvisational quilts, which I exhibited in two solo quilt shows at the museum art gallery. I was hired as an occupational therapist for a new mental health program, and while I waited for the facility to open, I cleaned staterooms on the BC Ferries ships and worked in an activity program for kids.

In July 1980, Bill and I got

I got married in an antique gown, and our hopes were as bright as the flowers on the cake and the patchwork sleeves on Bill's shirt.

I may have looked blasé, but I was thrilled to exhibit my quilts in 1979 at the art gallery of the Museum of Northern British Columbia in Prince Rupert.

married in a grand hippie wedding. I wore an antique lace gown, and his shirt had colourful patchwork sleeves. The hall was decorated with my quilts and with gigantic bouquets of foxgloves we had picked by the railway tracks. At the end of the evening, our friends waltzed dreamily around the floor, twirling Japanese paper umbrellas they had found in a storage cabinet.

We honeymooned at Salt Lakes. I had been trying to get pregnant for years and had undergone testing and procedures without success, but getting married seemed to do the trick. By autumn I was pregnant, feeling very happy and contented—until it all fell apart.

⁓⁂

By the middle of January, I was in constant, relentless pain that the doctor attributed to morning sickness and anxiety because I wanted a baby so badly. I silently endured until the end of January, then collapsed from massive internal bleeding. My world collapsed with me. Near death, I had an emergency operation that revealed a rare intra-abdominal pregnancy. Apparently, the fertilized egg had burst free of the fallopian tube and set up housekeeping outside the womb. Of course, the fetus could not sustain itself, and the pregnancy was surgically terminated.

I was devastated. I felt like a freak of nature, betrayed by my body and sabotaged in all my expectations. Bill and my mother sat with me day and night in the hospital, the strength of Bill's feelings anchoring me to life, my mother's quiet presence helping to restore me. Friends brought gifts and distractions—a handwritten book of poems, a feathery pin, a copy of *Bulfinch's Mythology*. I read that book obsessively. The bloodthirsty unfairness of the myths appalled me, yet it somehow brought me comfort to know I was not unique in my suffering and woe. My friend Margo hung a picture of a heron painted on Japanese rice paper at the foot of my bed, and I lost myself for hours in its graceful flight.

My body slowly healed, but my heart did not. Bill did his best to console and care for me, but when he began to crumple under the strain, I could not help or comfort him. Hollowed out by our experiences, we seemed to have nothing left to give each other, and began a very long, slow, sad parting.

I felt such a failure at babies and marriage. I needed counselling or a support group, but as an occupational therapist who had worked in psychiatric settings, I saw myself as a helper, not as someone who could ask for help. Instead of seeking the emotional support I needed, I moved alone to Salt Lakes to lick my wounds, feeling bitter and grieved. Angry at the world, at myself, at doctors, I cut myself adrift by drastically changing my lifestyle and giving up on my profession, my marriage, my conventional ideas of stability.

Recovering from a major operation, my stomach cobbled together with huge Frankenstein stitches, I was weak and weepy. In my first stint alone at the cabin in the late spring of 1981, I fetched firewood for the stove one piece at a time, tottering down the boardwalk like an old lady. It took all my strength to pull the boat in to shore, and rowing the short distance to visit my neighbours across the cove left me panting and sorry for myself.

Bill and I had bought the boat and cabin in such innocence and high hopes only a year before. Now we were separating, reconciling, and separating again. The cabin became my refuge. Weak in body and emotionally bewildered, I

My patchwork shirt proclaimed that I was a serious quilter, though I made up my own designs instead of following traditional patterns.

settled into my unlikely haven gradually, in bits and pieces, without facing up to my decision. I would stay a few days alone at Salt Lakes, then go back to Rupert. I'd return to the cove with a skiff-load of clothes and my rocking chair, then go back to town for hot baths and library books, for hugs and recriminations.

My first Christmas alone in the cabin was bleak, but brightened by a surprise my friends left—a stocking filled with Christmas treats.

It took a year or so before the little cabin was home to me. We both knew I intended to stay when I bought a treadle sewing machine. Bill backed the van down to the boat ramp, lifted out the heavy wooden cabinet and balanced it in the boat, then waved sadly as I took off. I intended to support myself by sewing. I didn't want to be an occupational

I moved to a cabin just above the rocky shore, with a wooden boardwalk where rounds of firewood cut from beachcombed logs were stacked.

Rowing the heavy Davidson skiff was hard work for me when I first moved to Salt Lakes, but it helped to strengthen my body and to calm my mind.

therapist any more—being competent and professional, taking care of other people's problems. I felt sour and cynical about hospitals, doctors, the "helping professions." I would be a quilter, a seamstress, a mender of fabric, not of lives.

Moving from town to Salt Lakes eased my overwhelming anxieties and fears. Instead of worrying incessantly about my shattered health, faltering marriage, and precarious finances, I now had real, elemental dangers to focus on: storm, fire, sinking, getting lost in the fog. But the quiet and fresh air soothed me; I grew stronger as I chopped wood, pulled the skiff in and out, and sank knee deep in springy pink and gold moss during long, exhausting, exhilarating muskeg walks.

I was warmed by the casual acceptance of my new neighbours who gave me fresh fish and invited me to breakfast, and to raunchy, raucous beach parties on the boulder-strewn shore. Their nonchalant and unquestioning support was of infinite value to me, both practically and emotionally. They didn't see me as odd; they were odd themselves. They didn't see me as an ineffectual failure, but as a greenhorn who could use a helping hand.

Salt Lakes

"Kriiis-tuuun! Cuuhhm foohrr dinn-neehrr! Briiing suuumm pohhh-ta-aa-tooehs!

Lorrie, Linda and Margo were my three friends at Salt Lakes, and tremendous friends to each other. Their cabins stood three in a row directly opposite mine, on the far side of the cove. They had perfected a deep, slow yell to get in touch with me. I'd grab my salad and the bag of potatoes, fasten my sagging door tight with a nail through the hasp, and head down the wooden boardwalk with my dog Arlo at my heels. I'd pull in the clothesline, an ingenious but often ferociously aggravating way to keep a boat floating in deep water. The clothesline had nothing to do with laundry. It was an endless loop of rope that ran from a pulley on shore to another pulley on a floating platform. Boats were tied to the rope and then hauled out beyond the low tide mark, or pulled in to shore.

Five minutes of rowing took me to the derelict dock in front of Linda's cabin, where I'd step carefully to avoid the holes, then cling tightly

The Salt Lakes dock is on the left. The cabins of Linda, Lorrie and Margo are in the middle of the photo. A fisherman lived in the cabin at far right.

to the handrail as I climbed up the ramp in the twilight rain. Arlo dug in his claws and scrambled after me. I'd skate across Linda's slippery wooden deck and open the door to a kerosene-gilded glow and the smell of boiling crab.

Meals were abundant and leisurely at Salt Lakes, accompanied by home-brewed beer, roll-your-owns, and endless Scrabble games. The smell of woodsmoke and creosote mingled with the acrid singe of wool socks hanging too close to the fire. Helly Hansen rain gear as thick and stiff as milk cartons and damp clothing with the faint sour reek of old dishrags added to the mix. Outside, the sweet savour of clean-washed air, cedar kindling, wild mint crushed underfoot. And rain, constant rain.

My three friends worked together cutting wood, painting their boats, and canning salmon. On canning day, huge tubs of salmon sat on the old wooden table under the cedar tree between Lorrie's and Linda's cabins. Lorrie was quick and practical, her butcher knife glinting in the sun as she slashed jar-lengths down the side of a silver fish, then sliced deep through orange sockeye flesh. "You want to leave the bones in for calcium," she said. Linda deftly filled jars, giving

Linda (top), Lorrie (middle) and Margo (bottom) lived in the cabins across the cove from me. They welcomed and mentored me as I adapted to my new marine-based life.

each a tap of salt, then wiping the rims, fastening the lids and stacking the jars. A massive pressure-cooker rocked and hissed on Lorrie's stove inside, another jittered on a camping stove outside. Margo, who worked in quality control at the cannery in town, went back and forth, supervising the boil with scientific precision.

Lorrie had left small-town Saskatchewan at nineteen, quitting her job as a Dairy Queen carhop and breaking off her engagement to her high school sweetheart. She joined Prairie friends who were heading west to find work. Looking back, she remarked, "I didn't really feel rebellious, but I guess I was. I liked it around Rupert, met people and befriended them, and they befriended me. I met Paul in a bar and he took me across the harbour on a snowy night. So romantic! We went up the slough on a high tide, up to the lake. It was incredible." Soon Lorrie was living in a little cabin at Salt Lakes, borrowing Paul's boat, the *Bathtub*, to get to her job at the post office in town.

Margo was a city girl, a biologist whose first job after university was in the Queen Charlotte Islands, now renamed Haida Gwaii, a distant archipelago 290 kilometres west of Prince Rupert. She lived with friends in a variety of remote rustic cabins there and became accustomed to boats, wood stoves, and harvesting the bounty of the seashore. When she got a job based in Rupert, she was drawn to life across the harbour, and bought the tiny box-like cabin beside Lorrie's, where she lived alone for over a year.

Linda had fetched up at Salt Lakes when she and her fisherman boyfriend "went for a drift," as she described her first trip across the harbour in a little flat-bottomed sailboat that didn't sail very well. "We ended up rowing into Salt Lakes. We didn't know anyone there, but we stayed the weekend. A year later we bought a cabin there and a boat called the *Sieve*." Linda grinned and said, "Not a bad boat except it leaked a lot, but I commuted back and forth to the cannery in that leaky boat until it self-destructed."

Later, Linda owned a sturdy gillnetter named *Naiad*. She expertly eased her thirty-foot fishboat to the dock, jumping lightly onto the slippery planks to tie the lines. She did the maintenance on the engine herself. A friend described her as "tremendously competent, working on the motor with huge wrenches while clouds of smoke billowed forth." When I asked Linda if she found running the boat intimidating, she laughed and said she didn't know enough to be intimidated.

Linda was seasonally self-employed, mending fishing nets at Salt Lakes. She had a swaybacked wooden net-float with long, waist-high railings that supported the vast swaths of gillnet. Grass grew in the cracks between the planks and around the plywood patches nailed over the biggest holes. The net-float was anchored behind Horsehead Rock in front of Stew's cabin, and in sunny weather, Stew would stand naked between the drapes of netting and play his saxophone.

Linda and Margo are mending gillnets out on Linda's net-float. The huge nets are stretched over the wooden railings, with the cork floats in a pile beside them.

Linda mended nets from morning to night in certain seasons. A gill-netter would tie up stern-first to the net-float, and unreel the net from a huge spool onto the float. Sometimes there were several fishboats out at the float, with fishermen lazily drinking beer and talking about fish. Linda enjoyed the company but was not distracted from her seemingly endless labour as she worked her way through the netting. Her net needle was steady in its rhythm—loop, catch, tighten—in a repeating sequence as she rebuilt the structure of the mesh.

Linda had a blue net-mending hat that her fisherman friend had bought in Vancouver's Chinatown. It came in a flat, saucer-sized case that Linda unzipped, taking out a small circle of nylon. Flourished in the air, it magically transformed into a broad-brimmed hat. The brim was stiffened with wire and could be coiled into concentric circles to diminish it for storage, yet spring forth to a majestic sixty-centimetre diameter.

It was lovely to row out to Linda's net-float on a warm summer evening, to lounge on a pile of nets while Linda worked and her friends enjoyed their leisure. The inlet at Salt Lakes faced southeast, so the sun would set behind us unseen. The windows of Prince Rupert across the harbour reflected the sunset back in an enchanting grid of tiny glowing red and gold squares.

But more often it was raining or blowing, and then Linda would have the net-float to herself. Without her friends, without her jaunty hat, she would stand hunched and enduring in the wind as water sluiced down the hood of her grey raincoat, her needle never ceasing in its loop, catch, tighten.

The Mystery of Life

My first winter at Salt Lakes was bleak. I was still frail and nervous, and everything took great effort. I remember how hard it was to turn over in bed under the weight of thickly layered blankets and quilts, and how my breath steamed in the chill air. I would struggle out of bed several times each night to shine my flashlight out the front window into the wind-driven rain to make sure my boat was still there. I'd put a few more logs on the fire and use the beautiful china chamber pot painted with roses that Bill had given me in better times.

The cabin had a huge, eccentric wooden bedstead that must have been constructed from a boat that never got built because the sides were slanted like a dory and the edges of the frame were gracefully curved. This peculiar piece of furniture fell apart shortly after my marriage did, and in my zealous chagrin at being on my own, I decided I didn't need a bed at all and instead slept on a foamy on the floor by the wood stove. I used the bed planks to build shelves with curving fronts to store fabric and quilting supplies, and turned the bedroom into a spacious sewing workroom lit by two dim propane lamps.

One of my first projects was a patchwork comforter filled with down from old sleeping bags. It lay so heavily on top of my many covers that I felt flattened, and I traded it for a stereo system that ran on car batteries. I didn't realize I'd have to take the heavy batteries into town to recharge them, so I soon gave up listening to music. I didn't do much sewing that first winter, but I finished a little crazy-quilt sunburst. Around the outer medallion, I embroidered a quotation that had struck me when I first read it: "The mystery of life is not a problem to be solved, but a reality to be experienced." I wasn't sure what this meant, but it comforted me.

I brooded and daydreamed through the long nights and short wet days, going to town sometimes to stay a few days with Bill as our marriage continued its interminable unravelling, as our feelings for each other snagged on knots of anger, tenderness, and remorse. I was in a quandary of contradictory emotions: I wanted to live alone and I was very lonely; I still wanted a baby and was alternately hopeful and terrified of becoming pregnant.

The previous May, I'd had a second operation to tidy up from the first, and the doctor dourly counselled against maternity. I went home to my parents in Seattle to recuperate, and as soon as I was able, I visited the

My precious treadle sewing machine sat in the corner of my workroom between a big table and my rocking chair. Propane lights and a window gave enough light to sew. Photo by Claire Tangvald.

university medical library there. In an obstetrical journal, I found statistics, freakish odds that I mulled over obsessively. One in five thousand pregnancies was ectopic, with only 01.6 per cent of those progressing to an abdominal pregnancy like mine. Infant mortality was 90 per cent in abdominal pregnancies, with congenital malformations likely in the remaining 10 per cent. Maternal mortality was 6 to 18 per cent.

But my momentum was still towards motherhood, and I'd seen so many doctors by this time that I had a wide spectrum of opinions to toy with. I clung to the advice of one doctor who felt that my first, doomed pregnancy was an unfortunate mischance that would not happen again. Extravagantly ambivalent, I veered wildly and unpredictably from hope to panic as I waited for my now erratic periods. I was getting physically stronger, but still had gnawing pains from scarring and adhesions, and my emotions see-sawed wildly.

It snowed and snowed that first winter at Salt Lakes. I'd never lived in such cold whiteness, though my friends from Ontario and Saskatchewan assured me the weather was mild. I worried that the weight of the snow would break through my fragile roof, and I climbed a ladder to get rid of it. I shovelled and scraped until I was exhausted, then sat on the roof in tears until a neighbour noticed me and came to help. The snow only lasted a week, giving way to rainy, windy, stormy days. If my friends were experts at snow, I was better at rain, having grown up in Seattle. I didn't mind the rain; it made me feel at home. My roof leaked, but the grey skies did not depress me as they did my Prairie friends. I was used to being wet.

The cabins of my three friends across the cove looked quite picturesque after a winter snowstorm.

Spring came, and I was often happy, content in the quiet peacefulness of my new home, caught by the careless green beauty all around and soothed by the nurturing sea. I'd take my breakfast down to the steps by the boat shed and sit drinking coffee and dreaming out over the water. My side of the cove was the quiet side, though my dog Arlo was a boisterous companion.

The opposite shore was livelier, with boats arriving, work parties cutting and stacking wood, friends gathering on the beach while laughter and music drifted on the wind. On Sundays, when everyone was likely to be home, I'd spend half a day slowly visiting around the cove, leaving home mid-morning to clamber along the steep bank of precariously balanced boulders that narrowed into the creek-like opening of the slough. Arlo, four-footed, was more adept than I on the slippery rocks bared by the falling tide. I'd cross a sandy beach past a couple of dead boats and a mysterious trunk half-broken and rotting on the sand, and head down the path that led to Linda's.

Linda would probably come with me to Lorrie's place. We'd spend hours sitting at Lorrie's table while she fed us toast and homemade jam. Lorrie had a round cast-iron lid retrieved from an old woodstove that she

Bubalina was a fine sea dog and happily joined Linda in her rowboat.

set on her propane burner. She'd lay two half-circles of rye bread cheek to cheek on the lid to toast, turning the slices with her bare fingers, then plucking them off for buttering.

If Margo hadn't already joined us, I'd move on to her house for a chat and a slice of the indescribably delicious bread she baked from flour she ground by hand. Then I'd stop at Stew's for a cup of tea and a philosophical discussion. Sometimes I'd take the winding hillside trail past Stew's outhouse to a tall, upright green cabin filled with top-heavy piles of tools and old engine parts, to consult with the harbour's mechanical guru. He'd offer me a home-brew and I'd tell him my outboard woes. We traded expertise—I mended his clothes and he kept my outboard motor running.

The daylight would be waning as I headed back down the beach. Linda might offer me and Arlo a ride home, since at high tide the opening of the slough could not be crossed. She had a beautiful little rowing skiff named *Stanley* that a friend had given her on condition that she keep its original green colour. "It's always been my favourite colour," Linda told me recently. Her eyes grew soft and reflective as she remembered, "*Stanley*, my very own dream boat and Bubalina my faithful hound, go hand in hand in my memories. Bubalina always sat on the stern seat while I rowed."

In the slowly fading light, Linda would row me home. I'd sit in the bow with one hand petting Arlo and my other hand stroking the smoothly sanded ribs of Linda's lovely little boat. I'd look past the steady rhythm of Linda's arms to see Bubalina smiling doggedly as the moon rose in the dusky afternoon sky and the water rippled in a silent shimmering vee.

Wild Parties

In the early eighties, the harbour community seemed to be in constant sexual upheaval. Couples often came north together and broke up, then tangled with someone new. In this casual free-wheeling atmosphere, people crashed together like billiard balls and often parted as quickly, seemingly without guilt or jealousy or remorse. When I first met the folks who lived at Salt Lakes, it was hard to sort out the couples. Larry and Linda were together, I thought, and Gene and Lorrie were a pair. But soon Paul and Lorrie were together, and after a while, Linda was living with Gene.

When the fishermen came in from fishing, Linda's tiny cabin was the site of epic parties, with gumboots and raincoats piled knee-high on the porch, and visiting boats tied three-deep at the dock. A canning kettle of crab would be cooking outside on the rocky shore. Larry would prepare a massive, intricate seafood dish, and Linda had to thread herself sideways through the gathering crowd to set plates upon the potluck table. There might be an abalone stir-fry, fresh-baked bread, a big slab of halibut, over-ripe bananas fried in butter. Larry once brought a case of champagne. Someone would always say, "I wonder what the rich people are eating tonight."

After dinner, the battery-powered stereo was cranked to full volume, and the plywood floors shuddered under dancing feet. The little tin airtight stove fell off its legs once because of the vibration, and a shower of sparks spewed out where it parted from the chimney. The dancers stopped long enough to reassemble the stove, then whirled and stomped with renewed vigour. As the kerosene lights dimmed, fiery courtships flared, and electrified pairs slipped off into the rainy, windy darkness.

Parties happened all around the harbour, with group hugs, dancing, and excellent food. There was a lot of warmth, with the wood stove on and twenty or thirty people all overdressed because of the weather outside. People took their clothes off, which always made a big impression.

I enjoyed the food and the dancing, but felt increasingly staid and unsophisticated as the reckless nights wore on. I timidly tapped my toe to a few mating calls, ended up in a few strange beds, but my sombreness and ambivalence kept me from full-fledged revelry or romance.

There had been parties even wilder than these, a few years before, parties that became part of the local folklore—the toga party, and the "orgy" in a back bedroom. Linda and Lorrie laughed, recalling them later. "After the toga party, there were a few people that weren't speaking to each other," Linda commented ruefully. Lorrie added: "Now I'm more aware of what my actions are, but back then you just did what you wanted to do." After the inevitable, unlamented break-ups, the lightning-struck lovers usually settled back into good-natured friendship.

~&

My own attempts at forming new bonds had been tentative and disappointing. The closest I came to a meaningful relationship was with a seventy-year-old man, a retired logger and fisherman who invited me to travel the coast with him. While my contemporaries were mingling and mating, I was voyaging sedately with the old captain, a wiry, white-haired gent with a fondness for young women. And I was fond of him. I felt taken care of, protected and appreciated. Enveloped in old-fashioned courtliness, I could ignore the brash sexual simmer that still seethed among my remaining single friends. Sailing away, I could overlook my chagrin as new families formed and flourished in the little coves around the harbour.

"If I was thirty years younger, what a pair we would make," the old captain would say, disregarding the fact that I'd have been in kindergarten. He admired parts of me that had never been praised before, especially my broad, square feet, so suitable for long hikes, and my sensibly wide shoulders and sturdy back. We went on lengthy and leisurely explorations of the coast between Rupert and Vancouver. I grew strong and healthy aboard his boat, rowing long distances, hiking on wilderness beaches, and roaming through hushed green forests breathing the pristine air. Living on a boat with an expert mariner, my nautical skills improved, and my own confidence grew.

But after each trip, I was eager to get home. I missed my cabin and doing things my own way. I missed my tiny garden and my quiet days of quilting. I missed my dog Arlo, now older than the captain if computed in dog years, but not welcome aboard. And I felt a bit ludicrous

The old captain's boat, *Chilco*, was as sturdy and seaworthy as he was.

with such an elderly suitor, isolated from both the frivolities and the serious concerns of my own generation, and farther away than ever from the possibility of motherhood.

So the captain and I regretfully and fondly parted company, and I went back to sitting on the sidelines, a reluctant wallflower in the coastal mating game, waiting for the lightning to strike.

Exceedingly Cautious

Salt Lakes was the wilderness to me, not uncivilized, but harsh and often frightening. There really wasn't much to be frightened of, except drowning, and nobody but me seemed to worry about that. It seemed that there were no wild animals nearby or dangerous people, no need to lock the door. In the frequent violent storms, the cabin shuddered in the wind with its flimsy walls shaking at each gust, but it stayed upon its pilings. I'd watch a tall tree swaying outside the window and imagine it blowing over in the gale. I could vividly picture my small home crushed and broken by a falling cedar.

I was exceedingly cautious lighting the propane stove, convinced it might blow sky-high and take me with it, and I was just as careful with the hatchet and axe, the flaring Aladdin lantern, the jar of mayonnaise cooling in the creek. I pored over first-aid manuals, underlining the sections on food poisoning, lockjaw, and uncontrolled bleeding.

Linda and her sweetheart Gene had moved to my side of the cove in the winter of 1982, into a tiny shack aptly named the Last Resort, which was as wide as a railway boxcar, half as long and nearly as dark. They added propane lights, built shelves and a lounging bench, lifted the side of the roof that faced the water to put in windows at eye level to their loft bed, and eked out a two-metre-square dining room.

I was glad to have neighbours. We worked together to repair the boardwalk and to rebuild the clothesline float and the water system, and we often ate together, inventing impromptu meals that combined whatever we had handy. The soft glow of their windows was a great reassurance to me on dark stormy nights.

Friends and strangers alike were generous with encouragement and advice. As I drifted helplessly on my maiden voyage in the new skiff, the propeller churning air instead of water, a fisherman yelled, "Put rocks in the stern." I rowed awkwardly to shore and

My tattered and well-used copy of *The People's Handbook of Medical Care.*

I was an anxious but determined boater, wearing my floater coat and a huge whistle as I crossed the harbour on a brisk autumn day.

piled the back end of the boat with boulders. When I pulled the starter, the bow of the boat rose abruptly in the air, with water slopping in torrents over the stern. "Put rocks in the bow!" he yelled, laughing.

After strangers towed me home when my outboard motor stalled, a friend showed me how to poke a little brass cylinder back into place so fuel could flow to the engine. Linda patiently tinkered with my plumbing and my stove, ingeniously adapting spare parts from Paul's vast collection of second-hand treasures.

Margo gave practical advice: shut off the motor when lost in the fog and listen for other boats and the sounds of town; don't cross the harbour in a storm on a falling tide; chain up the skiff at the town dock to thwart thieves. Lorrie showed me how to point my skiff at an easy angle to the angry winter waves, and taught me to bury scarlet starfish in the garden, to put wads of newspaper in wet gumboots, to read the tide table. I taught my friends the fine points of quilting.

I was a very nervous boater and was lucky to have Gene along the first time my motor stopped in a storm. Gene was lounging in the bow, face relaxed and tilted to the wind. I sat rigid in the stern, jaw clenched, hand fused to the handle of the outboard, eyes scanning each white-crested wave as the rain pelted down. The motor glugged and sputtered and died, and the boat rocked in the waves. "Oh no, oh no!" I moaned, rushing frantically to set the oars into the oarlocks, picturing us adrift, swamped, shipwrecked.

Gene didn't bother shifting from his languid slouch. "Calm down,

Lorrie seemed to revel in the wind and the motion of the waves as she steered *Vanessa*, her classic wooden skiff.

Kristin. You don't have to get the oars yet, we're okay drifting. Check the gas tank and the hose." The problem was the hose, kinked because I was sitting on it, preventing gas from getting to the engine. For years afterwards, whenever boating got scary, I mentally pictured Gene in the bow saying, "Calm down, Kristin. Everything's okay. Just calm down." His ethereal presence always helped.

~❧~

Approaching the dock at Cow Bay on my first solo crossing of the harbour, I saw a form floating face-down and very still in the water. I queasily told myself "it's only a mannequin from the Sea Fest Parade." A novice with the outboard, I couldn't manoeuvre closely enough, so I turned off the motor and rowed over. Touching the head, I could tell by its weight and substance that it was a real person. Grabbing the collar, I lifted the head out of the water. It was a woman.

She felt very dead to me. I hadn't the strength to get her aboard, and couldn't let go to start the motor, so I just held on, wondering what to do. "Help, somebody drowned!" I yelled at a fishboat edging for the dock. The men stared impassively. "Come help me! You *better* help me!" I screamed. I thought they would lift her into their boat. Instead, a man climbed into my skiff and rowed it to the dock while I clutched my motionless burden. He didn't want to touch her.

Emergency responders came to the dock, but failed to revive her. Later, I learned that she had fallen from the cannery walkway and had not been in the water very long. I have always wondered whether she would

I am enjoying a ride in Linda's skiff, feeling at ease because she was the captain on this windy day. Photo by Gene Logan.

have lived if I had reacted more quickly, if I had known what to do.

I sometimes put Lorrie aboard as my imaginary passenger, because her pleasure in rough weather was inspiring. I had watched her come into the cove in a storm one day, perched nonchalantly on the gunwale, the narrow rail that edged the top of her skiff. She was riding the waves, her slender form swaying with the motion of the boat. She seemed confident and at ease, as if she'd been in boats all her life, though I knew she came from the Prairies.

"Aren't you scared, out in weather like this?" I asked, meeting her at the beach. "I love it," she replied, her eyes shining, strands of long wet hair blowing across a glowing, exhilarated face. It was not until years later that she told me that "at first, I was definitely scared of the water. I would get spooked by close calls."

As the months and years passed, my skills and confidence grew, and I became a more relaxed boater, but I never lost my cautiousness, my sense that boating was serious business. I kept a Saint Christopher medal lashed to the gunwale though I wasn't a Catholic, and I kept a quote from John Millington Synge pinned to my kitchen wall:

> A man who is not afraid of the sea will soon be drowned, for he will be going out upon a day that he should not. But we do be afraid of the sea, and we do only be drowned now and again.

Stress Test

Sitting at Lorrie's one day drinking coffee, we took a stress test from a ladies' magazine that Linda's mom had given her. Lorrie and I scored at the
"no stress" level, but Linda's upcoming trip to the tropics raised her score by
twenty points. She had important chores to do before leaving; turning her
skiff upside down on her net-float and towing it up the slough; disconnect-
ing the black plastic hose that supplied water to her sink; climbing a ladder to
put a bucket over the stovepipe. Our low scores on the stress test didn't mean
that our lives were without stress. Rather, it was that the magazine quiz didn't
cover any of our worries and dangers: drowning, getting lost in the muskeg,
keeping food cold without a fridge, being run over by a freighter.

My life was very quiet, with vast stretches of time when it seemed that
nothing happened. Yet I was busy. I chopped wood, bailed the boat, daydreamed out the window as I pulled bright-coloured threads through the
layers of a quilt. I struggled with the plumbing, dug clumps of rampaging
mint from the garden patch, and took long meditative rambles through the
muskeg. I began writing a quilting book to teach others how to make quilts
the way I did, without following a pattern. Every two weeks, I went to
town to work a forty-eight-hour, non-stop weekend shift at a group home
for troubled teens. Sometimes I left Salt Lakes a day early if storms were
forecast, to be certain I'd
get to work on time if
the motor broke down
and I had to row across
the harbour.

⚓

The siding on my cab-
in was "newspaper tin,"
which shone in the rare
rays of sunshine. The
printer in town sold the
used aluminum printing
plates very cheaply, and
they were light and easy

White cedar shakes covered part of my cabin, and I
nailed shiny "newspaper tin" to the rest. Arlo is on the
boardwalk, which is covered with fishing net for traction.

My kitchen was small and cluttered, with open shelves. I had traded a quilt for the white wood-burning cookstove. Photo by Claire Tangvald.

for me to handle. I'd clean off the ink with a gasoline-soaked rag, give the sheets a good polish, and nail them up to keep out the wind and rain.

My home was just a big flat box split into two rooms, with a third tacked gracelessly in front. Everything was makeshift. The water supply was a long black hose, spliced and duct-taped, that snaked its way downhill from a tiny pool. The water was tinted brown, like strong tea, and tasted fabulously nutritious and wildly fresh. It was muskeg water that had seeped through the thick abiding moss to pool in secret bogs before it flowed past cedar roots and muddy sinkholes to the tiny creek that trickled past my cabin and emptied onto the beach below the Last Resort.

Maintaining the plumbing was an ongoing challenge throughout my decade at Salt Lakes, and I was usually pleased, at least for a while, when the system fell apart yet again, and I could revert to dipping water from the little creek behind the house. In the winter, the pipes always froze and split, so I'd crack the ice in the creek with an axe and dip up water with a brass pitcher I'd been given as a wedding gift.

My kitchen had open shelves of rough splintery cedar planks, and a smooth, well-sanded wooden counter. I soon learned to thwart the mice by storing all my staple foods in gallon jars. I traded a quilt for a wood-burning cookstove, but did most of my cooking on a two-burner propane stove.

The back half of the cabin was my sewing room, with a treadle machine, a big work table, and a quilting frame. It was dark and cold until a friend installed propane lights and I enlarged the doorway to the front room so heat could circulate. I traded my sewing for big windows that Gene helped put in. Most of my home improvements involved trades or favours from friends.

I wasn't eager to work in town, so I made quilts, wall-hangings, potholders, and patchwork baby hats to sell at craft fairs or to trade. Quilt-making was the one element from my former life that I transplanted and nurtured; the only thing that I excelled at, and a source of pride and competence. I was a good quilter, inventive and industrious, and quietly proud of my original designs. Sewing without electricity was surprisingly easy; I tried to put in four hours a day sewing, and quickly adapted to the vigourous rhythm of the treadle sewing machine. I didn't miss my electric machine except for zigzagging, but I mourned the loss of my steam iron and never found an acceptable substitute.

I needed to iron each patchwork seam, so I borrowed an archaic South American iron with a top that opened to insert glowing coals. Adjusting the heat was impossible and sooty smudges marred my sewing. My grandma gave me her mother's heavy old flatiron, which built up my biceps and kept me in constant motion, jumping up to fetch it off the wood stove, or to return it to the heat.

My roof leaked, had always leaked. Every summer I'd climb a ladder with a bucket of roofing tar and a spatula, to spread a thick black frosting on the asphalt seams. It never solved the problem, and finally friends offered to help put up a new roof. Loading the rolls of roofing, the sheets of plywood, the nails and heavy tar buckets into my boat was hard work. So was carrying it up the beach to the house, up the ladder to the roof. There were three stubborn layers of mossy old patchworked roofing to be pried up with bleeding knuckles and heaved onto the raspberry bushes below.

When the old roof was finally off, it started to rain torrentially, soaking my clothes and food and quilts and books. I tried to drape my home in plastic but it seemed hopeless. I retreated in tears to Lorrie's, feeling like the sky had fallen. Lorrie hugged me, fed me tea and toast, then handed me a heavy sterling silver oval. "Here, you can have this," she said. It was the hundred-dollar hair clip she had ordered from Des, who made custom jewellery. She had worn the beautiful hair clip daily until she suddenly cut her hair. My fingers moved over the deeply carved rosettes and intertwining Celtic swirls. "I'll just keep it until your hair grows out," I said.

When the rain stopped, I went back home. The water was already draining out through cracks in the floor, and evaporating in the sudden sunshine. The next day the new roof went on and I lit brisk fires in the wood stoves. I took clothes, quilts, and fabric to the laundromat in town,

Lorrie lived for a while at Casey Cove, where her caretaker's cottage was surrounded by the spooky Victorian-era buildings of a former marine station. Photo by Iain Lawrence.

ironed the wrinkled pages of my favourite books, and put away the buckets that had collected drips for so long. Over the years, Lorrie and I passed her silver hair clip back and forth, until it was finally lost.

⁓❧

In 1983, Lorrie left Salt Lakes to live alone as caretaker at Casey Cove, a gothically derelict collection of huge empty barracks, dusty work sheds, and Victorian-era officers' quarters. The complex had been built around 1915 as a Government Marine Station, and was now abandoned and subsiding into the mouldering landscape. Her tiny caretaker cottage faced the bleak, twisted, falling wreckage of a large wharf. Lorrie was truly alone—no one else lived there.

Lorrie made sails there, setting up her second-hand industrial sewing machine in the middle of a vast echoing wooden warehouse. She'd sweep the splintery floor and unroll endless lengths of Dacron or canvas from the bolt. She'd mark the dimensions of the sail with chalk, squinting in the pale light that filtered through the cobwebbed windows. When I visited, I'd help her guide the gigantic pieces of stiff, awkward fabric through the machine. Lorrie sewed in a rackety din, deafened by the cantankerous gasoline generator that supplied her sewing machine with electricity.

I enjoyed these visits, especially when the generator finally coughed to a halt and we'd walk on the beach or go berry picking, but I always felt uneasy as dusk obscured the eerie, empty buildings of the compound. This seemed a lonely, introspective time for sociable Lorrie, similar perhaps to my earliest days at Salt Lakes, a time to prove that she could take care of herself, alone. I was very glad when she moved back to her warm, friendly little home across the inlet from me.

Saltwater Baby Quilts

Margo was proud of the year and a half she lived alone at Salt Lakes. Feisty and independent, she moved into a leaky one-room cabin in October 1978 as the days were getting shorter, the storms were growing fierce, and the rain was pelting down. She had never run a boat or a chainsaw before, but she patched the roof and had the good sense to buy the *Cadillac*, a strong seaworthy wooden skiff that could manage the winter waves. "As a single woman, I had to be able to do certain things, or I couldn't live over there. I had to have faith in myself," she told me. She chopped all her firewood on the weekend so she could come home from work and quickly light a fire.

Margo was the only person from Salt Lakes commuting to town that winter. As a biologist, she sampled fish at the docks in town, and observed and documented the big fishboats. "Some mornings it would be blowing, pitch black, and not a light in any of the cabins," she recalled. "Nobody would even *know* if I got into trouble. A lot of the men were really macho, saying they liked it when it was stormy, when it blew really hard. I didn't like it! I liked it when it was very calm."

There was only one time she didn't go in to work—a day of extreme high tides, drenching rain, and howling winds: "A great storm, it really blew.

Margo's skiff, the *Cadillac*, was a splendid wooden boat. Seen here in a boatshed, it had been expertly and beautifully restored.

Margo and Han's cabin was perched on pilings above the shore. Firewood is stored under the porch, with uncut logs still lying on the beach.

Huge logs were coming in and battering the dock, so we used the *Cadillac* to tow the other boats up the slough." Then she and her neighbours spent the day protecting the dock by fending off logs with pike poles and peavies.

Margo met Hans, part-owner of a big factory trawler, when she went aboard as an observer to verify the catch. She courted him in her customary self-reliant way, going out to the ship anchored in the harbour, tying her skiff to the ladder, and climbing up to take him homemade bread. "Then I invited him for supper and he never left," Margo said.

Hans soon made improvements to the little cabin, setting up a generator to charge batteries and run a few electric lights. He built their wood stove himself, welding it from heavy metal sheets, adding a baking oven in the chimney and heating coils for hot water. Later, they had a little propane water heater with a pipe that ran to an outside shower.

Margo and Hans were a well-settled, married couple with a very functional, smoothly running home by the summer of 1981, when I became their neighbour across the inlet. Their cabin looked like a rustic dollhouse painted red with a playing-card roof, and it had amenities that I coveted: hot running water and electric lights, a glass-doored cabinet for wineglasses and Japanese pottery, a red-topped table that basked in the light from two corner windows.

Margo carrying Galen in a backpack as she hikes up the trail to the lake.

Margo was a weaver with no space for a big loom, so she used a table loom, moving it at suppertime. She served tiny gourmet dinners to one or two guests tightly packed around the little red table. She and Hans lived sensibly and elegantly, rising above the picturesque shabbiness of Salt Lakes.

In expectation of their first child, Margo and Hans built a little addition on the back of the cabin, and Hans rigged up a small washer-dryer to the generator. Margo seemed a calm and serene mother. Looking back, she recalled "my life then was so tranquil, but I did find it isolating. No one else at the Lakes had a baby, and my life changed drastically with the birth of Galen. Everyone was very excited about this baby, but all of a sudden, I realized that I was the only one that really had the baby."

Hans built a securely fenced deck next to the house where little Galen rode a red tricycle, wearing tiny red gumboots and a little yellow raincoat. I was charmed by Galen, by his head of electric dandelion fuzz and his clear, focussed gaze, by the seriousness with which he studied his world and the delight he showed in birds and waves, eggbeaters and outboard motors. He liked being on the water and was quite at ease in Margo's skiff, tightly encased in a little orange life jacket and strapped into an infant car seat.

With a baby right across the cove, I felt faint stirrings of angst, which I subdued because Margo was my friend and because I still imagined joining her in maternity some day. My friends were having babies and with each birth I faced contradictory feelings. I delighted in the soft, warm, cuddly infant, and wished it was mine.

⁓❀

Babies were being born around the harbour, and a new tradition evolved as we began making baby quilts as a communal activity. On quilting day at my cabin, the women came up the beach in life jackets, carrying steaming casseroles and bottles of wine, with unfinished quilts securely wrapped in plastic. Wendy from Crippen Cove and Wendy from Dodge Cove each brought a boatload of wet, cold, smiling women. Skiffs crowded the clothesline, and the porch was heaped with boots and rain gear. Women with glowing red faces exchanged chilly kisses and rubbed stiff hands by the wood stove. Quilts were unwrapped and the room exploded in colour.

When Margo arrived for quilting day, she tied her skiff to the clothesline and then pulled all three boats out to deep water before joining us.

Quilting days shifted around the harbour, and I spent many warm, peaceful afternoons quilting with my friends at Salt Lakes, Crippen Cove and Dodge Cove. I was the local quilting expert and was happy to pass on my techniques and give advice, but I didn't work on the first group-made quilt created by our saltwater community.

Lorrie, Linda and three other friends made log cabin squares for baby Tlell's quilt in 1979. "Nobody we know has ever had a baby before. This is a special event and we want to recognize it," Linda declared. The women asked my advice because they had never quilted before and the squares were of slightly different sizes, and rather crooked. I told them not to worry, to just trim the bigger squares or add a little extra to the smaller ones. One of the women recalls: "We slapped it together and it looked just fine, a little miracle." I was impressed that the women had worked together to create something so complicated and beautiful.

Lorrie showed me the thank-you letter from Tlell's mom: "The quilt is absolutely beautiful. I am feeling quite a bit of nostalgia. All kinds of memories are drifting through my mind. Tlell picked up on the excitement when we got the box at the post office and wheeled home through the pouring rain. I cried when I saw what it was. I can't stop staring at it! Tlell has thoroughly checked it out, having crawled to all four corners, then gotten up and walked around it in circles a few times, smiling and looking at the colours. Then she sat down, looking pretty smug. Thanks a lot for the beautiful quilt."

We secretly started a quilt when we learned that Margo and Hans were expecting a baby. Bill and Shelley from Crippen Cove had unearthed

Five young women who had never quilted before made log-cabin squares for baby Tlell's quilt. Although the squares were of different sizes, the quilt was beautiful.

a black and pink patchwork pinwheel made years before in one of their cabin-fever crafting sprees. I suggested that we each add a border around it, medallion style, as this was how I made quilts. A friend visiting from an island beyond the harbour sewed on the first border of blue velvet, and I surrounded it with a patchwork sawtooth border.

News of the quilt spread by word of mouth, and the quilt top travelled back and forth across the harbour as friends asked to work on it. Ghislaine bordered the medallion with striped fabric, then Lorrie put patchwork at the corners. Helen elongated the design, and Dolly finished it off with interlocking strips for the final borders.

"Pass-the-medallion" was how I described this casual and inclusive process of community quilting. We didn't plan the quilt or worry about what it was going to look like—each person added whatever she wanted to. As Dolly remembers: "We just used whatever materials we had. Nobody went out and bought new fabric for the quilt. We dug through our boxes to see what we had."

The quilt top kept growing until nobody else wanted to work on it. Then we sat in a patch of sunlight in front of my cabin to quilt it, and to embroider Galen's name, birthdate, and astrological sign on the blue velvet border. Multicoloured threads spelled out "Babe in the Woods," "Water Baby," and "Babe o' My Heart."

Margo recalls receiving the quilt: "It was a quiet spring morning with the sun shining on the cabin. Galen was just a few weeks old. Hans and I were drinking coffee and a skiff pulled up at the dock. A wonderful group of women with wide smiling faces came up the dock and across to our place. They brought this beautiful quilt and a bottle of wine. We were so surprised. And so overwhelmed. At eleven in the morning, we all sat on the porch and drank the wine."

For the centre of baby Yavonnah's quilt, Lorrie sewed colourful strips of fabric together to make a patchwork square, and Dolly framed it with a border patched out of bright triangles. Over the months, other friends passed the growing quilt top around, adding concentric borders. We were also working on another pass-the-medallion quilt for baby Morgan. Dolly started it with a pastel butterfly and others surrounded the butterfly with border after impromptu border.

Yavonnah, a bright-eyed toddler in a white lace bonnet, came to quilting day with her mother, Clara, and was given the quilt. Then Clara sat down to stitch on Morgan's quilt. She was an expert

The communal creativity of a dozen women (and one man) resulted in Galen's baby quilt. Photo by Julie Moore.

embroiderer and transformed the pale butterfly in the centre, outlining and embossing the wings with vibrant rose, pink, blue and gold satin stitch. Dave, who lived in town, came to stitch on Morgan's quilt. He enjoyed sitting elbow to elbow with the women, plying his needle and chatting. He was one of the first fellows to join the quilting circle.

Dave also participated in the Banana Moon quilt we made in 1984 to celebrate Lorrie and Paul's marriage. Linda remembers appliquéing the centre square: "It was meant to be a crescent moon, with stars around the outside, but it didn't turn out. It looked like a flag I'd made years before, when we proclaimed Salt Lakes a banana republic." We enjoyed the visual joke, because Paul was known for buying boxes of overripe bananas and drying them on racks above the wood stove. Six women and two men added borders around the banana moon square, creating our first full-size quilt.

Toddler Yavonnah is given the group-made quilt being held up by her mother, Clara, and Lorrie.

⚯

My friends were having babies, and I envied them, but I found an excruciating comfort in making baby quilts as a communal activity with the island women. I had already made innumerable baby quilts to

Dave joined Dolly and Ghislaine to add stitches to Morgan's quilt. He worked on several of the community quilts.

sell, and these didn't bother me; the quilts I made to earn money were just attractive arrangements of fabric, skillfully sewn together. In contrast, our group-made baby quilts had me sizzling with emotion, with misery and regret, until I could hardly sit still in the quilting circle.

But I could not stay away. The force of my yearning was too strong. I needed to make quilts with these women, for these babies; needed the warmth, the group-ness, the solidity of my friends. And they needed me, because I knew how to quilt, and because they cared for me. With each new baby and each new quilt, I felt a jealousy that I was careful to hide from my friends. It wasn't just the baby I wanted, it was that eternal triangle of mother, father, baby, and the stability and trust it implied. The warmth and connectedness of these new-formed families made me feel isolated, unpartnered, withering on the vine.

One baby quilt brought out the worst in me. I hadn't worked on the quilt top, but I joined in on quilting day. Elron's quilt was serene yet lively, with nautical touches that honoured his seafaring father, and welcomed his mother Sheila, a newcomer to the coast. The centre medallion was appliquéd with black satin dolphins cavorting on a denim square, surrounded by an anchor-printed patchwork border.

On quilting day, the women embroidered Elron's quilt with emblems that expressed their hopes for the new baby. Sheila, who had been invited to stitch on her son's quilt, embroidered a castle with a jaunty flag flying, a place to go in imagination and fantasy. The quilters stitched fish, crabs, and a seahorse to encourage love and respect for the sea, and a sailboat to inspire a voyaging spirit. They stitched smiling flowers and a beaming sun to evoke the bounty of nature. Like the fairy godmothers in the tale of Sleeping Beauty, the women wished the infant well. They were enjoying the day and their task, swapping delivery room stories and advice on teething as they sewed.

I was uncomfortably aware that my feelings didn't match the festive mood. Although I had looked forward to quilting day, I was now overcome with jealousy as I listened to the women talk about their babies. I sat quiet and remote, stitching my bitterness and grief into the cloth with each jab of the needle. My grim mood was heightened by the remembrance of the miscarriage I'd had a month after Sheila's baby was born, and by my mental re-hashing of the arguments Bill and I were having about divorce. These were subjects I did not bring up at the quilting table, but which evoked terrible and complicated feelings in me. I felt like the evil witch in the fairy tale as I contrasted my misfortune with the good fortune of my friends.

But as I stitched, I felt such a stab of anger and spite that I was at last forced to acknowledge my own wretched emotions. "It is plain wicked to feel like this. It is hurting me, it can hurt others, and it's just not right," I told myself. I sensed, irrationally, but deeply, that my poisonous ill-will could be transferred through the quilt to the innocent baby. "Stop it," I said to myself. "Just plain stop."

The 'Banana Moon Wedding Quilt' was given to Lorrie and Paul when they got married. This was the first bed-sized quilt we had ever made.

That day, I finally began to confront my own hardness of heart, and the damage I could do. I realized that either I had to stop quilting with my friends, or I had to stop feeling what I was feeling. I chose the quilting circle and kept on making communal baby quilts, enduring jealousy like a fever and fighting to dampen its flames. With each group-made baby quilt, my envy and hurt dissipated, my yearning lessened, and my sense that I had other satisfactions and blessings grew. Yet even now, and perhaps always, there remains a tiny, tender spot inside me, of distant, muted loss.

Sheila has become a dear friend to me, but it was many years before I ever spoke to her about what I felt on that long-ago quilting day. "I don't know why my feelings came out so strongly at that time," I finally told her. She looked at me and said: "Maybe it was safer to feel jealousy towards me. I was the outsider." Her memories of the quilting day for her son's quilt are very different than mine.

"I was new to Dodge Cove, becoming involved in Karl's community and a whole different life," Sheila recalled. "At first Elron's quilt was a secret. I knew about it, but I hadn't seen it. I was invited to quilting day and I got to quilt on Elron's quilt. I was thrilled. That was the beginning of a whole network of women friends and the many things we do together. That quilt is very special to me, very much part of that first year of being on the coast, when I was learning to run boats, and being a partner and a new mother."

Love and Fishes

Coastal courtship rituals were eccentric—spirited dancing in gumboots, the giving of fish, outgoing tides romantically ignored until a boat was left stranded on the beloved's shore. Offering to cut a woman's firewood was taken more seriously than an engagement ring, and the arrival of a baby usually solidified the union. Intentions were often declared at the annual erotic poetry contest where shyly rhyming love sonnets and bawdy odes to lust were read aloud to an attentive audience before the dancing began. In this era of wild parties and ricocheting romance, bonds sometimes formed that have lasted thirty or forty years. And when folks recount their stories, love, fishing and babies are often intertwined.

Dolly came to the coast as a teenager, working in the cannery and waitressing. She remembers her first boat ride: "A friend with a little skiff picked me up in town to take me to Dodge Cove. Her motor broke down in the middle of the harbour. It was a beautiful, calm, sunny day, but I'd never been

Dolly had a beautiful rowing skiff she named *Fern*, that she used at Crippen Cove and sometimes rowed to town.

on the water before. I was terrified! I thought—what does she know about motors and boats? We're going to drown out here." Dolly didn't drown, and was soon borrowing a kayak to get to Crippen Cove. She would put a shovel in the kayak and paddle over from town. "I dug up a big area, turned the whole thing over, and had a wonderful garden. I'd pick peas and take them back to Function Junction and shell them on the dock there."

Dolly met Alan in 1977 and spent time with him whenever he came in from fishing. Soon they were living together at Crippen Cove in a narrow two-room cabin where they would raise two children. "I didn't know I'd be living there so long. I thought it was temporary," she told me. She recalled her first sight of the cabin: "It was pretty tacky and primitive, very different from what I was used to. No furniture except an old table, an old closet. Nothing else but an old stove that badly needed repair. We collected rainwater off the roof into a forty-five-gallon drum. No electricity yet, no telephone, a little wooden seine skiff ten feet long with a Seagull motor. We were young; we didn't really care how little we had. We didn't think about it much."

Alan bought a fishboat, and Dolly went fishing with him. "I'd never fished before, but that was the big herring year, 1979; lots of people made money. We got back to town just in time for the Erotic Poetry Contest. We were ready for a party, and that's the night I got pregnant. That's what cemented our relationship. I went fishing when I was pregnant, but I couldn't fish the whole season."

The baby was born prematurely and named Leon, to give him the strength of a lion. He sometimes stopped breathing because his lungs weren't fully developed and had to be in intensive care. Dolly's voice was subdued as she said "he had to be in an incubator for several weeks, being fed with a tube. It got to me, watching the other mothers hold their babies, when I couldn't hold mine." She stayed at a friend's apartment in town until the baby was strong enough to be taken home to Crippen Cove.

There was no one else at Crippen Cove with kids, no one to give advice or support, so Dolly was glad

The tiny alternative community at Crippen Cove seemed serene and idyllic at high tide, when water covered the extensive mud-flats.

that Alan was home from fishing. "It's nice to have a fall baby if you're living with a fisherman. He's home the whole winter to help out. I washed diapers by hand at first, hauled water, heated it on the wood stove. After a few months we got a generator and a little washer-dryer that didn't work very well, so I'd often take laundry to town." Her second son was born in 1982. "Shawn was so big, twelve pounds. A very hard birth," Dolly recalled. But life at Crippen Cove was easier with her second child. By then, she had running water, electricity, a phone, and neighbours who also had children.

⁓₰

Shelley and Bill had left a conventional life in Montreal, searching for adventure. "We had heard stories about the north," Shelley says. "We were crazy, young and ready for anything. A friend took us across the harbour in a huge open skiff loaded down with six or seven people. The water wasn't rough, but it wasn't calm either." She had never been in an open boat before.

It was dark when they arrived at Crippen Cove. "We had to jump out of the boat and wade in knee-deep water to shore. I was horrified, the water was so cold! It was an adventure, a great adventure. Our friend took us to his cabin and gave us dry socks and pants; he served up a fabulous supper. Everything was terribly romantic."

Offering dry clothes to a guest is a north coast courtesy, as ordinary and thoughtful as offering a glass of cool water in warmer climes. Almost every house and cabin had a drying rack above the wood stove, often made from the slats of a baby crib rescued from the dump. Wet gumboots hung suspended upside-down, their wide soles caught neatly by the slats, and guests were expected to visit till their socks dried out.

In 1975, Shelley and Bill got a boat and moved to Crippen Cove to act as caretakers of a little Nordic-style house on a grassy point. Bill said, "My favourite memories are of going around in boats, of messing around in *Mud Puppy*." Looking back on her early life at Crippen Cove, Shelley says: "Those were my happiest days. It was more than I ever dreamed of, that little house, the solitude. Life was very simple. We had fun. We had a little sauna and would invite people over and serve huge dinners, then go take a sauna and roll in the cold wet grass. I was a city girl, and I was discovering a part of myself that I hadn't known was there, that was self-sufficient and courageous. I felt like I belonged. I'd wake up and every day was a treat."

Bill adds "but it was monotonous too." He laughs with a mixture of pride and embarrassment as he says, "I want to explain how we got into quilting. Do I look like a quilter? It started with cabin fever, a lot of time on our hands. We did batiking, weaving, spinning, natural dyes. I was making looms, we set up a spinner, had a treadle sewing machine. Shelley got a book on quilting, and I knew how to measure and cut and

Shelley, sensibly clad in her floater coat, seemed to delight in the waves as she crossed the harbour between Crippen Cove and Prince Rupert.

use the sewing machine. We had to entertain ourselves in a cabin with no electricity. Often, there would be only one or two other people at Crippen."

"I became much more solitary, went through a real personality change," Shelley said. "There were days when I didn't want to see people. It's strange. Maybe when you change your life, when you go through that transformation, part of you changes too. I was very naïve. I didn't know that my life up north worried and troubled my parents. Or I didn't care—it was a very selfish existence. I don't know if it was a deliberate choice, moving 4,000 miles away from my family, my roots. Maybe I was trying to escape the protective life that I knew so well."

Wendy and Des met at a Salt Lakes party in 1977. Des invited Wendy to visit him at his wilderness home in the far-off islands that stretched beyond the Prince Rupert harbour. She vividly recalled her first trip out: "I loaded up on supplies, enough for a few weeks and flew out there in a little float plane, my dog Rufus and I. Des was there, in this beautiful spot, and I was enthralled. I went out there to see what it was like and to see whether anything was going to come of it. We spent the winter out there quite quiet and lonely, yet not lonely, because I found it fascinating."

Wendy didn't realize how far from Rupert they were until they came into town, a day-long journey in Des's tiny sailboat. She recalled, "I hadn't been on the open sea before in a little boat. We were sailing, there was no motor. I felt at the mercy of all this. If I'd been alone, I wouldn't have had a clue. The boat's heeling over and Des says 'go hoist the jib' and I wasn't sure of which line to pull. He was trying to focus on the waves, the tide, the rocks. I was quite frightened that first trip."

But she went back, out to the one-room cabin with a loft. "The days were getting short; the cabin was dark. We'd light kerosene lamps at two-thirty or three in the afternoon and go to bed early so we didn't burn up all the fuel. We did basic things—fishing, baking, reading, crafts. A lot of time went into gathering wood, sawing wood." They were alone on this remote inlet the first winter, until two other couples moved there.

I had met Wendy when I still lived in town, before I moved to Salt Lakes. I couldn't understand, until I later began to travel by boat myself, why a book she had borrowed was returned wrapped tightly in three plastic bags. I wasn't yet familiar with the pervasive damp that accompanies a boat-based life in a rainy climate. Even after I lived at Salt Lakes, I didn't really experience coastal life as she did. To me, Salt Lakes was a rough and primitive world. For Des and Wendy and their few neighbours in the distant islands, Salt Lakes was just a maritime suburb of Prince Rupert, a pleasant place to visit when they came to town to buy supplies, pick up the mail, and socialize.

A whole day was needed for the forty-eight-kilometre trip to town in *Mere Nime,* Des's tiny, graceful sailboat with ancient, knowing eyes painted at the bow, the better to find the way in fog and storms. Sometimes, if the wind died midway, Des would row, standing up like a Volga boatman to add his body weight to each sweep of the massive oars.

Des and Wendy homesteaded in the wilderness for seven years, coaxing an abundant garden from the surrounding bush, raising chickens, supporting themselves with Des's fishing trips and with handicrafts they brought to town to sell or trade. Wendy spun and carded wool, dyed it in soft colours and knitted warm, chin-strapped toques. Des patiently tapped and carved and soldered, making intricate silver jewellery laced with Celtic designs. By choice, they lived far from the blessings of civilization and had a knowledgeable adeptness around boats and wilderness tasks that was in sharp contrast to my bumbling efforts.

Wendy and Des stayed at Dodge Cove for a month in the spring of 1981, awaiting the birth of their daughter, then went back to their cabin a week or so later. Wendy was nervous. "It was nice weather, but going out around the point, I suddenly felt an overwhelming responsibility for Bronwyn's life. I was going out to sea with this little baby a few weeks old. Not knowing how to handle a baby yet, and not being able to put her down to help Des with the sails or the tiller."

Wendy, Des and young Bronwyn lived in a small log cabin in the wilderness of the remote outer islands for seven years.

All the wilderness chores were arduous. Wendy washed diapers and did all the laundry by hand, and tried to keep up with the garden and bread-baking. Bronwyn's baths progressed from a wash bowl to a big round pan, then to a wash tub beside the wood stove, and on to the bathtub outside by the sauna. "At first, Bronwyn had a cradle downstairs, but then we netted off the loft for her. When she was nine months old, she somehow unlatched the netting and she came tumbling down. Pretty shocking. After that, she had a crib downstairs."

Wendy said, "We had a lot of time for her, for reading, playing, going to visit around the bay. She was comfortable in the skiff, sitting in the stern wearing her life jacket while we rowed out through the swift current of the pass to the outside beach where she took off all her clothes and ran around on the sand. Sometimes Maggie, who lived half a mile away, would bring her kids to visit. Bronwyn had friends, but when she was about three, she looked at a magazine picture of a whole group of kids and said, 'Mummy, where are there other kids?' She wanted to be with a bunch of kids like that. I said to Des, 'Maybe we should take her to town more.' She was fascinated with cars when we came to town, though she called them boats."

Sheila had come briefly to the coast in 1982, not intending to stay. But she joined up with the Sasquatch Tree Planters, a marine-based co-operative work crew that included Lorrie and Paul. They set off by boat, going north to plant seedlings on the steep slopes that had been scalped by logging. She told me, "I was just blown away by the people, the energy was so different than what I was used to in the Kootenays, where people were spiritual and political. The people on the coast were much more practical and at ease with physical tasks."

Sheila met Karl, a fisherman, the night the planters returned to Digby Island. They leapt into a whirlwind romance, and she went sailing beyond the harbour in his boat, *Tanleron*. "I got this incredible hit of the north coast, falling in love with the ocean and the lifestyle, and with Karl," she said. After a voyage to Haida Gwaii, they made a commitment to each other and moved into a little house next to the dock at Dodge Cove.

Their first child, Elron, was born in 1983, and when he was six months old, they decided to build a cabin in the remote islands. "We had a thousand dollars and we bought a whole load of building materials—nails, insulation, two-by-fours. We piled it in a herring punt and got it towed out. We lived on *Tanleron* while building the cabin. We made little fishnet playpens for Elron among the trees to keep him safe. After we had the platform up and the walls framed, he could scoot around in his little walker with wheels. He never crawled, but by one year's old, he was walking. We set up an outdoor bathtub-wash tub between the creek and the beach, with an open firepit beneath the tub, and a stovepipe to keep the smoke away while we were bathing. We'd haul water from the creek and have our baths in order, from the cleanest to the dirtiest. Then we'd throw in the dirty clothes and get out the plunger," Sheila said, laughing.

The cabin was finished in the summer of 1984, and Sheila and young Elron moved in while Karl went fishing for two months. "I didn't feel scared alone out there, even though I was pregnant again by that time; it was home. It was total magic to me, all this white rock and sculptured trees and clean water and incredible intertidal life. We were really just kids, playing out there in the woods."

⁓

"I never had a burning desire to fish, I knew nothing about boats," Karen said, telling me about the romance that changed her life. She was from the southern US, and had been visiting friends in Haida Gwaii. "Dave came to my friends' house, bringing them fish, and the rest is history," she laughed. She immigrated to Canada, married Dave, and deckhanded on his boat. "I had never fished before, but I thought it was a great way to make a living. We bought land with a boat shed on it in Dodge Cove in 1984 and built our house. We moved in, bought a new fishboat, and had a baby in the spring of 1986."

Karen handled the fishing gear when she and her husband, Dave, fished commercially off the west coast of Vancouver Island and in the waters of Haida Gwaii. Photo by Dave Prosser.

Baby Claire is watching through the wheelhouse window as her parents fish. Karen and Dave began bringing her on fishing trips when she was two months old.

Dave recalled his nervousness and indecision as Karen's due date and the opening of the halibut season drew near: "At the dock, people would say, 'Well, you have to go fishing, you just can't stay home for the baby.' But the farther away from the dock we got, the more people were saying, 'Well, you can't go fishing! You're not even thinking of going fishing, are you?' I didn't know what to do. I really wanted to be there for the birth, but that halibut opening was a huge chunk of our income, half the year's earnings."

"We decided to go for a bumpy boat ride to hurry things up," Karen said. "That day the water was just flat glassy calm, but we went anyway. All the halibut boats were coming into town, so we buzzed up the harbour, bouncing down the wakes of the boat, having a wonderful time. Claire was born two days later, and Dave was there for the birth. Before he went halibut fishing, he and the deckhands came to see me. The deckhands stood at the foot of the bed smiling, while Dave danced around the room in a hospital gown and gumboots, with this tiny baby on his shoulder."

Dave and Karen went fishing with Claire in the remote waters of Haida Gwaii and off the west coast of Vancouver Island when she was just two months old. "Adjusting to a new baby is hard enough when life is just normal, but it's really hard when you are putting in sixteen-hour fishing days. Working from dark to dark. I remember going to nurse her and just dozing off myself. We weren't into torturing ourselves, but if it was possible to fish with a baby, we wanted to do it. You talk to the old people, the natives, that was just what they did, went fishing with the kids and family. They told us that taking a newborn on a boat was easy, because babies don't do much, just sleep and eat and dirty their diapers."

Dave built a little bed for the baby across the foot of their bunk, and put extra windows in the back of the wheelhouse when Claire was a toddler, so she could watch the fishing. She learned to keep her balance on the rocking boat by going into a squat if she felt herself falling.

"Not many people our age fished with a baby, at the time we did it," Karen told me. "We didn't know anyone. A lot of people said we were nuts, they kept warning Dave that he'd have to change his fishing style. And he has, he takes her into account. We go to the beach for barbecues and walks, we see the spectacular places, and the amazing scenery of the west coast of Haida Gwaii."

Dave and Karen wanted to raise their little girl with a healthy work ethic, with the knowledge of what was involved in earning money for ballet lessons and new toys. At age six, Claire was given a dollar a day for helping on the boat. By age ten, she was receiving a "share," a small percentage of the profits. "Claire earns it," Karen said at the time. "She fetches and carries—she can get a number eight hook if asked to. She makes lunch sandwiches and helps with supper. She's been cleaning fish since she was five, and is very thorough and careful. Now other people tell us that's what they wish they had done. They wish they had gone fishing as a family, that they had taken their own kids out fishing when they were small."

Salt Lakes Forlorn

Margo, Hans and little Galen left Salt Lakes in the summer of 1984. All their belongings were carried laboriously down the beach and packed into crates on a barge, then two skiffs tugged and towed the barge to Dodge Cove. "Everything we owned was on the barge," Margo recalled, "and I was nervous. I was sure we were going to crash. But Hans navigated it very well."

I went along for the barge ride and was almost struck by lightning, or so Hans and Margo believed. "The sky grew really black; you could hear rumbling. It was pouring rain, and everybody was soaked," Margo told me, remembering that day of near disaster. "Your hair was really wet, but little wisps started to stand up around your head. And you were acting goofy and silly in a very serious situation because of the weird electrical fields around you. By then, your hair was standing straight out. We felt that a lightning storm was imminent and told you to sit down and stay low. You laughed,

As caretakers of the CBC transmitter site, Hans and Margo lived up on the hill in the house in the clearing beside the radio tower. Their boat is tied to the dock. Photo by Margo Elfert.

but sat down and stuck your head in a rubber tire that was used as a bumper on the barge, and your hair went right down."

The barge and its electrically charged passenger arrived safely at Dodge Cove, and the next day a helicopter picked up the well-packed crates and carried them to the top of CBC Hill, where Hans and Margo were to be caretakers of the radio transmitter site. "We had loads that almost didn't get off the ground," said Margo. "I had weighed everything on bathroom scales as I packed it, but with a couple hundred boxes I got a little off with each one, and the total weights went way over."

But it was all safely hoisted and trailed across the sky, then lowered onto the helipad on the broad green lawn by the radio towers, and friends carried boxes and tools and furniture into the house. "It was amazing! From the stuff we had in that tiny two-room cabin, we filled every cupboard in a very spacious house and had to build shelves in the basement."

They were quite isolated, alone on the hill, surrounded by meadow and trees, with a glorious view from their living room windows of the harbour entrance and the shadowy, mountainous islands beyond. In the opposite direction, out the kitchen windows, they overlooked the tiny village of Dodge Cove, a twenty-minute hike down the hill. When they first moved there, Galen couldn't walk up or down by himself, so Margo carried him in a backpack. "We would go down the hill to pick berries or go to the beach. If

Kids from Dodge Cove hiked up a forest path to celebrate Galen's birthday in the house on CBC Hill.

Galen wanted to play with friends in Dodge Cove, then I had to pack him up and take him down."

Linda and Gene broke up in the fall of 1984, and she moved to a communal household in Vancouver, renting a tiny room—a former pantry just big enough for a dresser and a narrow bed. She kept her cabin and came north occasionally, but never again would she really live at the Salt Lakes. She travelled alone in Southeast Asia, Australia and New Zealand for almost two years, then settled into a three-room apartment in a low-rent district of Vancouver.

Linda had joined a growing crowd of folks who were heading south. Countless friends and acquaintances, the saltwater people who had helped to make me feel at home across the harbour, were giving away their kerosene lamps, kicking off their gumboots, and high-stepping towards the bright city lights. This migration caught me by surprise. I hadn't imagined how quickly the tiny society that sustained me could change. Bill and Shelley and many other friends moved to Vancouver in the mid-eighties. Dolly and her family went to Vanuatu in the South Pacific for a two-year stint with CUSO, a Canadian aid organization.

Richard has loaned his herring skiff to help Shelley and Bill move from Crippen Cove. Lorrie is enjoying the ride.

Stew moved to Prince Rupert after a terrible accident. With enormous energy and enthusiasm, but not much real expertise, a dozen people had tried to fix the rickety, broken-down dock at Salt Lakes. We lashed sections of the dock together with second-hand rope and struggled to put new float-logs under the sinking walkway and get the ramp roller back on its tracks. To lift a log into place, a rope was thrown over a high beam connecting two pilings, and a tug-o'-war line of men heaved at the rope with all their strength.

I watched the rotten, worm-eaten pilings as they swayed with each pull of the rope, watched the beam as it shivered against the sky. "That looks really dangerous," I timidly said. "That wood is really rotten…." The men, ignoring me or unable to hear my voice, strained their muscles against the rope. Suddenly the beam snapped, arcing downward in a sickening swoop and hitting Stew a tremendous blow that knocked him flat on the dock, where he lay motionless. We thought he was dead, until he groaned and opened his eyes.

We were afraid his back was broken, but he could move his arms and legs, so we gingerly shifted him onto a padded plywood stretcher, wrapped him up for the trip to town, and loaded him into the most reliable skiff. He was in the hospital for a long time, eventually recovering, but deciding not to return to the rough and arduous life at Salt Lakes. He found a house in town, and rented rooms to his friends.

I sometimes stayed at Stew's house if the weather was bad, paying seven dollars to spend the night. I enjoyed the sociable buzz, the hot water that poured so generously from the tap, the big pot of soup that simmered on the back burner, the visiting children rolling their trucks across the rugs and tucking their dolls to bed under the sofa. At times, the house was full of pregnant women. Lorrie and Paul rented a room at Stew's the winter of 1984, waiting for Elisha to be born. Wendy spent time there as her belly grew big with the twins she was carrying, and Sheila, pregnant with her second child, was sometimes there for a night or two. Stew's house became a warm and friendly home-away-from-home for the saltwater community, but one more cabin stood empty at Salt Lakes.

Lorrie and Paul got married in 1984, and baby Elisha was given a wonderful quilt made by Paul and Lorrie's families. Our circle of quilters was intrigued, as we'd never seen anything like it. It was made of squares and each person had contributed whatever they wanted. Some of the squares were patchwork, some were appliqués; others were painted or embroidered and a few were simply plain fabric. It was a surprisingly witty and elegant

I'm having a cup of tea with Lorrie before taking reluctant Purrsilla home to live with me.

quilt, sensibly single-bed size instead of the traditional tiny baby quilt. Elisha's quilt became the inspiration for many of our future creations, which we called "Anything-Goes" quilts.

Lorrie and Paul moved back to Salt Lakes three months after Elisha was born, and their cat came to live with me, banished because of Purrsilla's unnerving habit of lying on the stairs above the baby's crib, staring at the infant with predatory intensity and swiping angrily downward with sharp, spiteful claws. Carried into my boat, the creature made a ten-foot leap back to shore, but was captured and imprisoned in a large covered basket. Arlo fell in love with the outlaw cat and would follow her moonily about the cabin with his tail wagging, until Purrsilla, enraged and exasperated, would turn with a nasty hiss and scratch his nose.

These were not easy months for Lorrie. "It was hard living at Salt Lakes with a baby," she said. "And I was working too, counting salmon at the fish plant in town. I'd commute to work with Elisha in her life jacket and backpack-seat in the middle of the boat; I'd drop her off with Marge on the Barge, our babysitter." Marge was a warmly maternal woman who

Lorrie heading to town in her skiff with her baby strapped to her chest.

lived with her family at the Cow Bay dock. Lorrie would spend her lunch hour in the crowded little cabin on Marge's barge, nursing Elisha and eating her own lunch, then rush back to work. Returning to Salt Lakes at the end of the day, she'd put Elisha to bed and get ready for the next day.

In the fall of 1985, Lorrie and Paul moved to Crippen Cove, to the big house that Bill and Shelley had built, to a life with electricity, plumbing, phones and computers, and most importantly, neighbours with kids. The last of my special Salt Lakes friends was gone. In the ceaseless falling rain, the three-in-a-row cabins across the cove seemed empty and forlorn, even after other people moved in. The rain fell and my mood matched the weather. Bleak, cold, lonely.

A spectacular view of the cove at Salt Lakes frames Elisha as she eats supper in her high-chair.

The Strong Women of Crippen Cove

There are photos of four women at Crippen Cove, each with her sleeve rolled up and her arm bent like Popeye's to reveal a bulging bicep. Strong women, and proud of it. Like men, they seemed to take pleasure in their strength and to be exhilarated by physical effort. Unlike men, they didn't take their strength for granted.

Tiny, elegant Shelley had been one of the first females in the Labourer's Union. "I didn't last very long, lifting and carrying fifty-pound bags of lime or sulphur," she recalled. "I don't know how I had the strength to do it. It was sheer will power over actual muscle." She worked with Bill to build their house. "I did the nailing on the roof. I got up on a scaffold for the first time, a narrow board up on the steep, high roof. I was afraid of heights; I spent too much time looking down, just hanging on. But I was determined to do it."

Life at Crippen Cove routinely involved hard work. Dolly wrestled with huge tree stumps to create new garden space, and dragged gunny sacks of seaweed up from the beach for fertilizer. When Alan came home

Shelley, Dolly, Nancy and Chloe take a break from cutting firewood to show off their muscles.

The salmon Dolly is holding probably weighed more than her son Shawn. There are more fish waiting to be canned.

from fishing and filled the bathtub with salmon, Dolly would spend the day, or the night, canning fish. She'd heft each slippery, unwieldy carcass onto her cutting board, lift the heavy, hot pressure cooker on and off the stove, carry five-gallon buckets of fish guts to bury in the compost pile. The next day she'd look grey with fatigue as she lifted kids, groceries, and laundry bags out of the skiff and carried them up the slippery low-tide shore.

Crippen Cove had changed over the years, yet somehow remained the same, a sociable, hard-working community. By 1985, energetic newcomers were building houses and boat sheds that dwarfed the original tiny cabins of the cove, using lumber they had salvaged from the abandoned Sunnyside Cannery on the Skeena River. The cannery owners were planning to burn the buildings down, but Marie, Ginger, Christiane and their partners showed up first with crowbars and chainsaws to dismantle the buildings and haul the precious lumber away.

Marie, who moved to Crippen Cove in 1984, remembered with pride and excitement the hard, dirty, dangerous work of tearing apart the cannery, which perched on high pilings above the fast-moving Skeena River. "I revelled in the power of my body, in muscles that worked, pushing myself to the limit. We were working in the rain and my hands were steaming from my body heat, from my own exertion in the cold. I got a real kick out of being physical. It felt really good to be strong, to do things besides lounge on the beach being a beach bunny, a party girl." Hoping to use her muscle profitably, Marie tried to become a longshoreman, but the union, a thoroughly masculine institution at that time, refused to grant her membership until years later.

Ginger had better luck. She trained as a carpenter and joined the United Brotherhood of Carpenters, then worked on renovation and construction projects in town. She and her family lived in a tiny high-ceilinged cabin at Crippen Cove, and were slowly and laboriously building a large addition around it using lumber from the cannery demolition. Ginger was a lithe, small-boned woman whose strength was in her sinews and in her determination to be strong. In dusty jeans and a leather apron, she looked deceptively girlish, until you watched her sawing planks or swinging a hammer, and noticed the strength and adeptness of her tightly muscled arms.

In the summer of 1986, I spent a few days working hard at Crippen Cove myself. I had borrowed a generator and a float moored out in the cove, and I spent excruciating hours grinding old paint and fibreglass off my skiff. A fisherman had told me: "Your boat will treat you as good as you treat it." After years of carrying me around the harbour, protecting me in storms and gales, and blessing me with quiet moments of beauty and pleasure, my little yellow lifeboat was leaking and needed my care.

My back ached as I bent over my upturned boat, trying to control a strong-willed sander. I was blinded by a haze of fibreglass dust spewing from the sander, choked by the acrid stench that penetrated the black rubber snout of a stifling face mask. Straightening from my crouched position, I felt heroically strong and proficient, part of the Crippen Cove work ethic.

I was glad when the generator ran out of gas and I could stop sanding for a while. "Krriss-tuun! Cuuhm foohr teeee!" floated faintly in the sudden hush. Friends smiled and waved as I paddled a borrowed rowboat to the front steps of Marie's small, narrow cabin perched on pilings above the beach. Dubbed "The Shoebox," the tiny house had a main room and a walled-off bed-sized alcove. A huge, half-built greenhouse-bathhouse six metres high and with more floor space than Marie's home, towered mirror-like on the slope above the cabin.

Marie's neighbours were sitting outside on the deck, which was her summer living room, her workspace, and a favourite place for the cove children to play. Two toddlers dropped kindling through the planks to the beach below while their mothers quilted a pass-the-medallion quilt with an embroidered teddy bear in the centre.

Years later, Marie told me how worried she had been when she was asked to help with the embroidery. "Ginger had chosen stretch terrycloth to use for the background fabric, because it was so soft. I just dreaded it—if you knew anything about sewing, you wouldn't pick this fabric to embroider on. My mom had taught me to sew, she's European, with a tradition of sewing and embroidery, so I knew the right way. I was a sewing school conservative."

Marie's cabin, the Shoebox, looks smaller than the woodshed behind it. The buildings sit on pilings above the beach at Crippen Cove. Photo by Garry Sattich.

Ginger and Marie chat and drink tea as they stitch on a baby quilt in a crowded cabin. Photo by Christiane Chouinard.

Marie laughed, "It endeared Ginger to me, to see someone so innocent actually tackling a baby quilt with such difficult fabric. I was used to patterns, and at first, I thought it would be really awful to work with this free-wheeling group. But I began to enjoy their approach: 'This fabric looks nice, so who cares how appropriate it is! Just make a quilt even if you don't know anything about sewing!' It appealed to me as an adventure, and I thought, 'these Crippen women need my help. I better help them,' so I showed Ginger and Wendy how to sew."

Christiane, for whom the quilt was made, has another memory: "Just before Elize was born, I visited Ginger and she was embroidering a little bear. She said it was for her niece, so when the quilt was given to me later, it was a big surprise. I wasn't part of the quilting group yet; I didn't realize that the women did this. Elize's quilt was secret until the presentation, and that's quite tricky in a small community like ours. Afterwards I got involved in other quilts being made."

Dolly and Lorrie had lassoed each newcomer into the quilt-making web, and informal quilting sessions like the one on Marie's deck tightened the threads that bound the tiny community, as well as linking them to women all around the harbour. Wendy, who moved to Crippen Cove the same spring as Marie and Ginger, remembered, "The first time I quilted was about a month after I came here. Elize was a new baby and it was her quilt. It was really nice to be included in the quilting circle and gain new friends." By this time, our community quilts had involved perhaps twenty-five folks from Salt Lakes, Crippen Cove, Dodge Cove, and town. We usually had several quilts slowly ambling towards completion without deadlines, guidelines, or quilt-guild bureaucracy.

Tiny wavelets splashed against the pilings that held up Marie's home, and yellow sunshine filtered skimpily through grey clouds as the women slowly stitched. Lorrie told us about a letter from Chloe, who had lived at Crippen Cove for several years before moving east, to an island across from Toronto. We had sent her a baby quilt, and she had unwrapped it on the ferry as she returned home. "She hugged someone she didn't even know," said Lorrie, laughing. "She was so overwhelmed by the quilt she couldn't believe it. So she talked to a

The Teddy Bear quilt for Elize was made by five women at Crippen Cove. Ginger embroidered the centre, with help from Marie. Photo by Carmel Pepin.

Ginger holds a strip of red fabric up to Marie's growing quilt top, trying to decide what the next border will be, while Sheila is quilting on Gabriel's quilt. Photo by Marie Meynen.

stranger, a woman sitting next to her. She had to tell someone that we had made this quilt for her baby, Cato. She was so excited that she hugged this stranger!"

Many of the squares in the "anything-goes" quilt had been made as reminders of Crippen Cove. Wendy made a sailboat, Marie a bright rainbow, and her partner Les, a husky piledriver, stitched a bird in flight. Carol appliquéd a white skiff with bright pink gunwales and a pink outboard motor, tied to a bright pink mooring buoy, with a smiling sea monster swimming by.

Carol explained the quilt square: "Wooden skiffs are highly individual, with their own history and character. Chloe had a carvel-planked skiff called *Heathen*, and she painted the top plank and the outboard hot pink for her own aesthetic reasons, but also to discourage theft by young macho fellows looking for a joyride."

My mind drifted to other quilts, other responses to our communal gifts. Our friend Helen had written to us after she moved from Dodge Cove to the American Midwest. Although the baby quilt we had mailed to her was made of abstract crazy-quilt designs instead of pictures or symbols of coastal life, it had evoked vivid remembrance and emotion. Helen wrote: "I shed a few tears when I opened up the box. The quilt is so beautiful, smelling of woodsmoke, that wonderful, forgotten aroma, and so brightly coloured, a relief and a joy to eyes sore from the repetitious pastels of conservative Illinois. You'll never guess the strong, passionate feelings that quilt arouses in me. Thank you. I'm afraid it will be a long time before Siobhan will sit still long enough to listen to her mother's tales of north coast life. But for me, that life is a constant reality, and I feel so honored and pleased to have such beautiful evidence of my life there. Your quilt has really made me happy, and caught me by surprise."

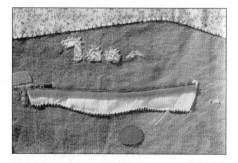

For Cato's quilt, Carol made an appliquéd version of his mother's skiff with a happy sea serpent swimming behind it. Photo by Julie Moore.

Sitting in the late afternoon sun drinking tea with my Crippen Cove friends, I watched calloused fingers grasping needles, rough hands smoothing soft fabric, strong arms tugging gently on coloured threads. These robust, vigourous women might not fit the stereotype of the dainty, ladylike quilter, but their quilts embodied warmth, love, and caring in a practical as well as symbolic way.

Coming in from the Wilderness Islands

The saltwater community stretched beyond the boundaries of the Prince Rupert harbour to sparsely settled islands where the only link to civilization was the radio telephone. Sheila and Wendy loved the faraway islands, the enchanted isles where they lived in a time out of time back in the 1980s. There was wistfulness in their voices—and pride and excitement and regret—when the women spoke of their years on the wilderness islands. The forsaken islands, for the women and their families had all moved away and their cabins were empty.

In 1983, after living for five years on the shore of the remote inlet, Wendy felt restless. "I was getting a little dissatisfied, wanting more of an income," she told me. "We didn't have money, just enough for basic subsistence—supplies and fuel. I came back to town, wanting to work, to get away for a while, to think about where I was going, what I was doing." She smiled ruefully and added, "Then I went back to the islands and got pregnant."

Wretchedly ill with morning sickness, Wendy returned to town until bleak, cold January, when she went back out and struggled with wilderness chores: "I remember being pregnant and trying to start the chainsaw." In the late spring of 1985, expecting twins, Wendy and Des and Bronwyn moved to Dodge Cove to be closer to the hospital in Prince Rupert. They planned to stay a month or two, until the babies were born, but the family lingered, because Wendy was ill after the births and not eager to be doing laundry by hand in a washtub for two newborns and a four-year-old.

The following spring, Wendy was invited to a Dodge Cove quilting day to help stitch on the quilts for her twins, Thora and Rheannon. She wasn't really surprised, since she had been sewing with the quilting circle for several years. "They were beautiful spring-coloured quilts," she recalled. "It was really neat to work on them. And it was a pleasure to tuck my sleeping babies in with their colourful quilts."

The family still talked of moving back to their wilderness home, of building an extension on the cabin and buying a generator for electricity. But as Wendy said: "By the spring, I was putting down roots and was more interested in staying in Dodge Cove than in going back to the wilderness

Wendy and Bronwyn in Dodge Cove rowing *Penny*, a skiff Des restored with yellow cedar, gumwood, Ace of Spades, and rivets made from copper pennies.

cabin. Des understood why, but he was in a different frame of mind. He had worked so hard building that place up. There were long discussions. The next summer we went out a couple of times, but I didn't travel much with the twins." Bronwyn started kindergarten, and the family settled in at Dodge Cove.

~❦~

Sheila was happy in the distant islands, living in the small, sparse cabin that she and Karl had built. It smelled of fresh wood shavings and woodsmoke, of drying herbs and homemade bread. She came to town for the birth of her second child in January 1985, then returned to the cabin with baby Brandin. Sheila and Karl liked the isolation, the wildlife, and the beautiful, abundant shore. They worked hard to sustain themselves and were proud of being self-reliant and resourceful, but after only two years, they decided to move away. Sheila's feelings about leaving were tumultuous.

"I felt like we had failed," she said. "I had fantasies that the islands could become something for us, where we'd live, maybe have a scallop farm. We moved because we were looking after a friend's fishboat, and it was too hard to take care of it in the winter out there. We had other reasons too. But I was so upset."

After they moved to Dodge Cove in January 1986, Sheila studied aquaculture and marine biology, wanting to learn how to make a scallop farm work. She got involved in the community quilts, hosting a quilting day for Wendy's twins' quilts, contributing a dazzling centre square for Claire's quilt, and setting up the communal quilting frame in her living room.

Friends would drop in for tea and an hour or two of quilting, but sometimes Sheila stitched alone: "I remember a winter's day. It was my turn to have all the Dodge Cove kids at my house, and it felt like at least eight kids, but maybe it was only four. I had my Walkman on and was quilting all alone, with all these little kids around. I did a lot of quilting on Claire's quilt, because it was set up at my house. It was the only time I really enjoyed quilting, because I had time to focus on it and to plan. But I always loved patchwork."

Karen is holding Claire's quilt. It started with a large centre square and grew as borders were added, becoming much bigger than our usual baby quilts. Photo by Garry Sattich.

On a visit back to the cabin, Sheila was surprised by the gift of a quilt for her son Brandin, by then three years old. Maggie, who lived at the head of the wilderness inlet, had been given the unfinished quilt top. She was tremendously frustrated by the task of working on the quilt. As she told me later, "I don't sew! Except for utilitarian purposes like mending or taking in trousers for the kids. I was given fabric along with the quilt top but had no idea what to do with it. It was in July, the busiest time of the year. I borrowed a sewing machine, but it was hard to sew, because the quilt top wasn't square. But I finished the quilt and hiked to Sheila's to present it."

The heart and the star in the corners of Brandin's baby quilt symbolize the love and friendship stitched into this unusual quilt. Photo by Carmel Pepin.

"It was most memorable getting Brandin's quilt," Sheila recalled. "Maggie trooped over to my place with her kids on a low tide, a major trek. She had to navigate a path that is a treacherous rapid on the high tide, so she came at low tide. She met me in the woods and said, 'I have something to give you.' She was so excited and happy about giving me the quilt and we walked back to my cabin."

Maggie showed Karl the quilt. "He received me at the door with open arms. It was a quiet, special moment. Karl and Sheila were very touched by the quilt." Maggie laughed and said, "But the really touching part is that I don't do quilts; I don't sew, the fine arts escape me."

Looking for Kids

Obsessed with the idea of somehow having children, I answered an ad in a magazine from a man who described himself as slightly eccentric, an engineer with a small son and a large boat he had built himself. He didn't seem odd when we met, looking tidy and respectable in a plaid shirt buttoned clear to the collar. Aboard the beautiful fifty-foot sailboat he lived on, he introduced me to his charming and extremely well-behaved six-year-old son. He then quizzed me on my sewing skills. Could I make covers for the cushions on his settee? When I told him I could, he asked, "With piping?" He served a limp salad and Kraft Dinner, and as I was washing up afterwards, he showed me how he liked to have his toaster polished. When we went for a walk, he kept his hand firmly on the back of my neck.

Later that evening, he unbuttoned his shirt and invited me to stroke his tattoos, which started at the base of his throat and continued to the soles of his feet. He was completely covered in provocative intertwining designs and was disappointed that I didn't want to get tattooed. We soon decided we were unsuited for each other, though he was reluctant to give up on such an expert seamstress, and I was saddened to say goodbye to his little boy.

I wondered if I could adopt a baby. In theory, the answer was yes—a single person could adopt. In practice, it seemed unlikely, as my income was very low, my living situation was peculiar, and babies were not readily available. Foster parenting with older children was suggested instead. As I filled out forms and sat through interviews, I pictured my life transformed. The kids would soon love me, and I, of course, would love them from the start. I'd be wise and caring, nurturing them from my vast, untapped store of maternal warmth and tenderness. I eagerly imagined myself as Mom.

The two sisters who came to me for the summer had not imagined being with me at all. They were First Nations kids who wanted to be with their real parents, whom they loved, despite alleged ill-treatment. They did not want to be foster children living in a small, unkempt cabin with a stranger, and they weren't happy to be stranded across a broad and forbidding stretch of water staring at the unreachable houses of town, where their parents were, where they longed to be. At that time, I wasn't yet aware of the infamous "Sixties Scoop," the government-sponsored removal of

Indigenous children from their parents. The Scoop was still active in Rupert into the eighties at least.

The girls liked me, but they didn't love me, and I reproached myself for not having warmer, more loving feelings towards them. But we grew accustomed to each other and had fun picking berries and making jam, reading stories aloud, poking in tide pools on the beach. They petted and hugged old Arlo and dressed indignant Purrsilla in doll clothes to act out long intense dramas, threatening and cajoling until the cat leapt from their cradling arms.

My nurturing was in small doses: braiding their long silky hair, bandaging knees and small hurts, tucking them into bed at night. I worried intensely that they might come to harm. They never seemed safe enough, whether playing on the beach or prancing down the boardwalk in trailing skirts and second-hand, high-heeled shoes. I zipped them into life jackets and took them to Crippen Cove where bemused friends welcomed my instant family and advised me on child-rearing.

I tried hard to be a good parent, to provide order and structure for the girls. But I was involved at this time with a man who liked partying, a musician who built huge bonfires on the beach and hurled songs at the moon, then slept until noon the next day and started again. My plans for a nutritious supper would be forgotten in favour of hot dogs at a beach party; bedtime would be postponed when we heard the music and hurried to join the circle around a blazing fire. I'd bring marshmallows and extra sweaters, and we'd sing happily in the endless summer dusk. As it grew dark, I worried that the girls might be sneaking sips of beer.

They were angry children, often infuriated with me and with the social workers who had broken their lives apart. But when they returned from family visits in town, they were often mad at their parents as well. The little cabin too frequently echoed with arguments, sobbing and slammed doors. "You're not our mother. You can't tell us what to do," they would yell, then threaten to steal a boat and run away. I wavered between permissiveness and inflexibility as I grew increasingly frazzled and uncertain. The girls became more frustrated and short-tempered with me and with each other.

September and the start of school brought new worries. For a while, I loaded the sleepy, sulky girls into the skiff and took them to school in town, then returned home to a disrupted day. Sometimes they weren't at the dock when I went back to get them, so I'd make anxious phone calls and search through the shopping mall or sit fuming in my boat until they appeared. We would head across the harbour in a twilight that came earlier each day, eat a quick supper and rummage in dim corners for school books and clean socks. The next morning, we would all be cranky and out-of-sorts.

I was in a quandary. The school board wasn't eager to pay for the school ferry to pick up only two children at Salt Lakes, but taking them to school in my skiff would be unsafe, if not impossible, once the October storms began. I looked unenthusiastically at apartments for rent in town, but wasn't sure my fragile relationship with the girls would survive transplanting. Teaching them myself at home by correspondence school was another possibility, but not an appealing one, given the way we already quarrelled.

When I told my problems to the social worker, she suggested a different foster placement in town. We talked to the girls, who agreed. They were a little sad to leave me, but pleased to go back to town. I felt wretched at the failure of my maternal experiment, yet relieved; I was suddenly let off the hook.

That fall, I was stuck in the doldrums, feeling flat, dull, aimless, becalmed. Each time I moved the furniture, I found bits and pieces of the girls: lost tiddlywinks, scraps of coloured paper, a dusty Barbie dress, pink plastic hair clips by the dark mirror. Crayoned drawings of elegant princesses smiled from their masking-tape prisons on the backs of doors. Foolish bright-coloured packages of Kool-Aid sat beside the coffee; a forgotten shoe stood ceremonially upon a shelf. I missed the girls. And I was also glad that they were gone, though I didn't like to admit it. I wasn't Mom. I was a flop as Mom and I felt a cringing, embarrassed disbelief at the fiasco of my summer charade.

Salt Lakes was almost empty now—all my good friends had moved away, while I held on like a limpet or a sea slug to a barren rocky shore. The jolly fishermen, the brave adventurous women, the optimistic hippies who had welcomed me were gone. The musician's charms had faded completely; the beach fires had flickered and died. The only people left were a few grizzled, disillusioned, hard-drinking guys and me.

Late one night I was startled by a distant shout for help coming from across the inlet. I snatched up my coat and flashlight and ran down the boardwalk, fumbled with knots, and started the motor, heading into the dark towards the unnerving cries of "Help me! Help! Help!" that echoed off the far shore. A man was flailing and cursing in the water a metre from the dock, just beyond the reach of his half-tied boat, his half-empty bottle. He must have fallen in while coming home from the bar in town.

He was extremely drunk. I grabbed at him and pulled at his arms; he got a leg over the side of my boat and I yanked him in. Reluctantly, I took him to my place, knowing that twenty minutes in cold northern water can cause hypothermia, a fatal lowering of body temperature. Hoping he wouldn't die, I decided guiltily against the recommended treatment which advised joining him in a sleeping bag for a warming skin-to-skin transfer of body heat.

Instead, I wrestled him out of his wet clothes and into my own long underwear and wool pants, into layers of socks and mufflers and sweaters. I packed him with hot water bottles, wrapped him in every blanket and quilt I could find, and abandoned him by a roaring fire. In the middle of the night, I heard him get up and open the door to my room. As I lay astounded, he stumbled to the corner and peed copiously into my wicker clothes basket, then shambled back to his pallet and fell asleep again. He woke the next morning with no ill effects from his ordeal, no sense of remorse, and apparently no memory of his late-night voiding.

Utterly vexed, I mulled over this experience, which seemed symbolic of my expectations and my folly. I quizzed myself relentlessly. Why was I living all alone in a derelict, almost deserted, backwater, inhabited only by a few irresponsible, unreliable, drunken, oblivious men? Why was *I* the one who had to rescue *them*? Who would rescue *me* if I was ever in trouble on the water? Why was I still at Salt Lakes, the only woman left, too stuck or too stupid to leave?

I briefly pinned my hopes on a man in town who had a thirteen-year-old daughter. She didn't seem to like me, but I liked him, and we started spending time together. I figured that the daughter would gradually become used to me, that I'd slowly win her affection. His apartment was very tidy, and he apologized when I opened the fridge one day and noticed a mandarin orange sitting on a clean white plate, growing a decorous fuzz of green mould. It was for his daughter's science fair project on the growth of moulds and fungi.

The mouldy orange didn't bother me. I was used to food rotting, to the wafting of powdery mildews and the spread of iridescent slime. I had toadstools growing in the cracks of my porch.

"I have lots of mould at my house," I told the man. "I could bring her some." Returning home, I packed a basket with a generous sampling of the many fungal growths that flourished at Salt Lakes, including some unusual mushrooms and a variety of mosses for decoration. The basket itself was perfect, having grown a delicate filigree of mould after lying outside by the woodshed all winter.

My gift looked very pretty in a barbaric way, and I took it to town imagining how grateful and admiring the daughter would be, how she would begin to like me when she won a prize at the science fair with the rare specimens I had given her. But the girl didn't value my offering, barely looked at it, and didn't thank me. The father smiled politely as he wrapped my basket very tightly in a double layer of plastic and thrust it to the back of the fridge. Somehow our romance faltered after that.

I decided to spend the winter in Prince Rupert. The housemother at the group home where I worked left on a lengthy trip, and I stepped into her shoes in the late fall of 1985. Monday to Friday, I lived with my dog and cat and five or ten teenagers labelled "pre-delinquent" by the authorities. On weekends, if the weather was nice, Arlo and I left Purrsilla sulking morosely in the big white building, and crossed the harbour to spend a day or two at my cabin.

My main duties were cooking, cleaning, shopping, spending meal-times with the kids, and being available for nighttime problems and emergencies. The teens were foul-mouthed and mad at the world, overactive or amazingly lethargic, older than their years but rather touchingly childlike behind their sophistication. The group home was noisy, chaotic, and not very private, and being the housemother there was a bracing antidote to my romantic fantasies of motherhood.

One of the attractions of my job was the room I was given, a spacious white-walled chamber with huge windows, a large table, and a lovely shining bathroom. For several years, I had been struggling to write a how-to quilting book in the perpetual semi-darkness of my cabin, and here I had electricity and space to work seriously on the project in my spare time.

I enjoyed living back in the town I had left so sadly four years before. I didn't have to chop firewood or slide down an icy beach to untangle the wet, dripping clothesline and bail out my boat. I played board games with the teens, tried to teach them how to quilt, and joined them at the movies and the swimming pool. I was still feeling a little raw from my recent experience as a foster parent, but I got along fine with the teenagers in the house. My emotional expectations were lower, my feelings not as involved. It was just a job, I told myself.

One evening I was hurrying back to the group home, carrying a big Christmas parcel from my parents and thinking about family, about men, about the kids I didn't have. Suddenly, unexpectedly, I was struck anew with my ancient feelings of grief. My upwellings of grief and loss had lessened in frequency, seldom coming to the surface anymore. On the rare occasions that my old emotions bubbled up from the depths, they had an almost nostalgic quality. Oddly, the hurt never diminished in intensity, returning sharply each time, and I was as inconsolable as ever. But now it lasted only a moment in time, the space of a breath or two, where once it had seemed to last forever.

Hearing voices, I snuffled back my tears and called hello as I came into the backyard. Two boys greeted me from high in a tree, dark shapes in dark branches in the dark night. As I sat on a bench to look for my keys, a third boy drew near and took my parcel and my knapsack. I was still wiping my eyes, and he asked me why I was crying. "Things in my life that happened a long time ago, that I was remembering tonight," I told him as he held open the door.

"That's a bummer," he said. His awkward sympathy was strangely touching. Standing in the crowded entryway with its rows of jackets and jumble of shoes, I gazed at the tough, rebellious teenage boy who had noticed my pain, and I thought, "this is what I have. Moments of closeness with children who are not my own." And I began to accept that it would be enough.

Quilts of Sunshine and Shadow

"Sunshine and Shadow" is a traditional quilt pattern composed of squares divided diagonally into light and dark triangles. Our group-made quilts were not traditional, but they expressed sunny sentiments until 1989, when two quilts that had been started in bright hope became symbols of sorrow. In the years that followed, most of our quilts were still made for happy occasions, but some held shadows, being made to comfort and console.

Shelley and Bill left Crippen Cove and moved south to Vancouver in 1985, and our friend Ghislaine mailed us a startling quilt square, made of interwoven red and green plaid ribbons, edged in a flurry of white lace. Her note said: "Here's a crazy psychedelic square to start a quilt for Shelley's new baby."

Lorrie surrounded this odd, bright centre square with star-printed blue satin, followed by a band of bright yellow, then Marie put on a red border printed with apples, oranges, grapes and bananas, and Christiane added a green border. I was excited by this giddy medallion with its wild exuberance and offbeat fabric. I sewed broad swaths of green and red plaid taffeta around the four sides of the medallion to echo the centre ribbons, and sent the quilt top back to Crippen Cove.

I was disappointed when I saw the quilt top again. Although it was still beautiful, its vitality had somehow been dulled by the blue brocade triangles sewn around it. The combined efforts of the Crippen women had been needed to attach the heavy blue brocade upholstery fabric, which crawled and slithered and stretched as it was being sewn to the lighter fabrics of the inner medallion. Marie, Lorrie, Ginger and Carol each tried in turn to sew it down. Finally, as Marie explained, "We tackled it with intense basting and got it on. But then it looked boring."

But by the next time I saw it, the quilt shimmered with renewed glamour and verve. Lorrie and Marie had rescued it from boredom by stitching giant lightning-strike zig-zags of yellow and red on top of the troublesome blue brocade. "It was pure inspiration," commented Marie. "We thought it needed something to jazz it up, to give it a gypsy caravan feel."

At an all-day quilting potluck, the women stitched comet-tails on the star fabric, outlined brocaded flowers with bright threads, circled apples and

Mia's baby quilt is spectacular, with bright colours, embroidered stars, and a dramatic zig-zag that evolved to enhance the design. Photo by Marie Meynen.

oranges with loop-the-loop stitches, and embroidered their initials on the back.

The finished quilt was sent back to Ghislaine, who had made the small centre square of ribbons. "It was really wonderful to see the transformation from beginning to end with totally different ideas and influences of all the people showing through," she said. "When I started it, I didn't have a clue what was going to happen." Ghislaine presented the baby quilt to Shelley and Bill.

"I was overwhelmed when I received that quilt," Shelley said. "We had just moved to Vancouver, a big step, leaving a small community and coming to the harsh city. It was very hard adjusting, and I was pregnant and about to have a kid. I was happy to be having a baby, but it was also a very lonely experience for me. Receiving the quilt, I went from feeling disconnected to knowing I still had all the connections that I had made up north. All the friends that loved me then still loved me, they still cared for me and Bill." Bill added that "it was really an emotional thing to get Mia's quilt. So many people had worked on it; the amount of work is unbelievable. You appreciate how much everyone put into it."

Years later, Mia's quilt, still in pristine condition, hung on the wall of her bedroom. Shelley said, "I was a little protective of that quilt because I didn't want it to get ruined. I'd have been upset if the baby threw up on it or made a mess on it. I'm hoping that it will last forever, and Mia will be able to pass it on to her children. I still get a wonderful warm feeling when I look at that quilt."

Lorrie and Paul moved to Vancouver after living a year at Crippen Cove. Paul was eager to trade in his wool pants and scratchy long underwear for a three-piece suit, but Lorrie wasn't as thrilled about the move. She consoled herself by thinking of all the friends who had already moved to the city. They had a grand giveaway before they left, bestowing books, boat gear, kettles and clothes with their accustomed generosity. Lorrie gave away boxes of fabric and unfinished quilting projects, but kept her treadle sewing machine. In Vancouver, she gathered Linda, Shelley, Margo, Ghislaine and other friends into a new circle of quilters.

Our northern circle missed Lorrie, and two quilts were started for her when we heard she was pregnant. Sheila found an unfinished hexagonal medallion that Lorrie had given away, and began building a larger quilt around the medallion, imagining Lorrie's surprise at receiving a baby quilt with a centre that she herself had sewn. At Crippen Cove, Marie and Wendy made a second quilt for Lorrie, of simple corduroy rectangles in soft, glowing colours.

"We just wanted to make a quick quilt to give her when she had the baby," Marie recalled. "We thought it would take too long to organize everyone to work on it. When we started the quilt, we didn't know anything was wrong. By the time we finished it, things were terribly wrong with the baby."

Marie's voice wavered, remembering this. "When we started the quilt, we didn't know that Gabriel would be so sick. When we heard that he was terminally ill, we had to decide whether we should still give her the quilt. Do you give quilts for sick babies? There was no Emily Post etiquette book to look it up in. We decided that she was our friend and that our present was just a sign that we thought about her, like a condolence card. She could hide it away or burn it, if that helped her to deal with losing a baby."

Our small community had never dealt with such sorrow before; our previous baby quilts had celebrated happy occasions. We felt sad and awkward and uncertain now, and nobody volunteered to work on the quilt that Sheila had started. I did a little quilting on it, but didn't have the heart to continue. Sheila finished it herself and mailed it down to Vancouver, where Gabriel was struggling for life, his frail spirit tethered to respirator and heart monitor.

Marie took the corduroy quilt south to Lorrie. "I was really scared!" she told me. "I hardly slept the night before. I was eight months pregnant myself, and I knew she spent every day at the sick kids' hospital, so I had my heart in my mouth. I didn't look forward to it. When I got there, I held Gabriel and saw how beautiful he looked, but how very sick he was. The fear left, and I felt an overwhelming tenderness for this small fragile human, but afterwards it affected me. It was just really tough, but it felt good that we'd made the quilt because you could see that Lorrie really appreciated it."

I remember visiting Lorrie at the hospital, where Sheila's medallion quilt was draped over the bars of the high white crib. Three-year-old Elisha climbed carefully into the crib and tenderly circled her arms around her baby brother, who lay limp and ethereal on top of the corduroy quilt. "I was spending all my time at the hospital, and it was wonderful to have those quilts," Lorrie said. "Gabriel spent quite a bit of his short life lying on top of the quilt that Marie and Wendy made."

Gabriel died at three months of age. His sister Elisha chose "Twinkle, Twinkle, Little Star" to be sung at his memorial, where poems and photos and prayers were placed on top of his quilts in the centre of a circle of friends and family. His uncle Ned wrote this song for him.

> Hear his silent song, it lingers on and we may follow
> Feel his mystery, beyond all joy, beyond all sorrow!
> Gabriel comes to tell a story beyond knowing
> Gabriel, all is well, your message is still growing
>
> See the glowing babe, his name is Gabriel the singer
> Know the shining one, he is the sun, the message bringer!
> Gabriel casts a spell, knowing he will win us
> Gabriel, all is well, your message grows within us.

Looking back, Lorrie said "the quilts were very healing. They were healing for the people who gave them, as well as to us receiving them. Both of Gabriel's quilts were very important in the healing process, and in being part of Gabriel's life and death. They represent Gabriel to me, you know. I don't fold them away. I keep them out, and keep Gabriel."

Grant missed out on a baby quilt, so we started one for him in 1988 when he was eight years old. He sorted through boxes of my fabric, picking lush velvets and satins, wild batiks and gaudy prints, not the more sedate fabrics that his mother Ginger had envisioned. "I wanted to use his baby clothes and spaceman pyjamas," she said.

Progress was slow. I started the medallion by putting blue satin and green velvet strips around a large heart-shaped motif cut from African dashiki fabric that Grant had chosen. Ginger struggled to add her borders to the asymmetrical shield-shaped medallion that I passed on to her. She framed the sides in another of Grant's fabric choices, an orange polyester with sinuous, snaky vines, and then added an emphatic geometric print at top and bottom. A friend gave her black velvet for the next border and helped her sew the first strip. But the slippery velvet was hard to sew onto the slithery polyester, and the lopsided shield was difficult to square up.

"I probably put on a strip a year," Ginger said. "I felt frustrated by the difficult fabrics. As a beginner at sewing, I had to do a lot of seam ripping." Meanwhile, the little boy grew into a lanky teenager, and in 1994, his family decided to move.

Two weeks before Ginger moved south, the quilters at Crippen Cove rallied to finish the quilt. Dolly helped square off the black velvet, then

Ginger added a patchwork border of triangles cut from the flannel space-man pyjamas she had saved for so many years. For the next border, she chose stretch terry cloth, "because it was the material I had, and it matched."

Marie and Wendy helped her attach the terry cloth border and were still joking about it two days later. "She really knows how to choose them. The fabrics are always hard to sew." Dolly added, "Marie likes a challenge in sewing, so we were all happy she took it on and we didn't have to do it." But the beige terry cloth border was perfect, an elegant, nubbly, matte backdrop for the exuberant centre. Sandy cut strips of corduroy for the final borders, "with a rotary cutter!" as her friends admiringly exclaimed, and the Crippen women layered up the quilt.

I came to help. To prepare for quilting and to finish the borders at the same time, the quilt top was placed upside down over the batting and backing. The edges were stitched, leaving a gap so we could reach in and turn it inside-out like a pillowcase. "We can just iron the edges while the quilt is lying on the rug," I said, a method I often used. Dolly plugged in the iron and started pressing the edge.

"Holy smoke!" she suddenly yelled. The clean, crisp corduroy of the outer border had an arc of yellow emblazoned on it, and Dolly's brand-new rug had an iron-shape melted across its yellow flowers. "How awful I felt," Dolly remembered. "Here's this beautiful quilt we had just finished, and I wrecked it."

I felt terrible too, for having given such stupid advice that caused damage to both quilt and rug. The women nervously laughed and joked to keep us from feeling even worse. The mark on the rug disappeared with brisk rubbing, but the mark on the quilt did not. The melted rug fibres were permanently imprinted on the turquoise corduroy. The women made suggestions: we could embroider over it, or paint it, or appliqué something else over the mark.

Unable to think of a solution, we continued with our basting and had a glass of wine. The afternoon was ending, but I wanted to quilt a few stitches since I might not have another chance. The women asked me to wait until the basting was done, but I had to get home before dark, so I barged ahead with my line of quilting, outlining the heart in the centre, and thinking how much I was going to miss Ginger.

By the next day, Dolly had hidden the iron mark by sewing new fabric over the corduroy. Wendy at Crippen Cove recalls that the cove children joined their mothers to add quilting stitches: "I was trying to encourage them to sew straight lines around the patchwork triangles since that seemed simplest, but they wanted to do their own thing, and they stitched hearts, faces, stars, and other designs." Even the smallest kids sewed a couple of wobbly stitches. The names of the quilters, young and old, were embroidered

Janice, Marie and Dolly are stitching on Grant's quilt, which was started with fabrics Grant picked out when he was eight years old. It was finally finished when he was fourteen.

on the back. Then Marie took the quilt to Dodge Cove so the women there could do more quilting.

I was tickled by the changes in the quilt since I had seen it two days before. Marie had invented an entirely new quilting technique by outlining the central medallion with an oversized blanket stitch. Her large, well-spaced stitches through all three layers of the quilt strengthened the fraying seams and gathered the blue satin very slightly to create an embellished, light-catching surface.

Beautiful purple fish now swam up the new side borders of the quilt and hid the yellow mark left by the ironing fiasco. As Lou outlined each fish with meticulous stitches, I described the disastrous mistake that had led Dolly to add this new border. Francine traced around a geometric motif with bright-coloured embroidery thread, while Sheila's stitches travelled down the undulating black vine in the orange border, giving it a 3-D sculpting. Karen's needle lassoed twirls of thread to put a French knot in each tiny flower of a paisley border. My stitches trudged stolidly along the seams, because I wanted to reinforce them against fraying. We all embroidered our names on the back.

The next day, Ginger took the quilt to Prince Rupert, and the quilting continued with town friends. Ginger too made French knots in the paisley, though she hadn't noticed the French knots that Karen had made.

We seemed to do a lot of our quilting on the floor. The backing, batting and quilt top for Dory's quilt has been layered up, and Jane is basting it together before we start quilting it.

Working on opposite sides of the quilt, on opposite sides of the harbour, both women had had the same idea. Ginger said she was going to give the quilt to Grant as soon as they were in their new home, even though the quilting wasn't finished. "I'm going to surprise him and put it on his bed when he goes to school. I can take it off every day and keep on stitching. He's waited long enough for his quilt."

Dory was an artist, a potter, and an adventurous woman who had tended remote lighthouses and then settled in at an abandoned fish cannery in the outer islands. The quilt we made to give her courage to endure cancer treatments reflected the esteem and affection that the saltwater community felt for Dory. Iain and I started it in 1996, hoping that a few friends would join in to quickly make a small wall-hanging to express sympathy and caring. Iain painted the central image of two dolphins, and I sewed a brightly coloured octagonal frame around it. I took this small medallion down to the Dodge Cove women before we left on our summer of sailing.

In the fall, Francine and Marty came up the hill and spread the medallion out on the sun-lit grass. It was now a metre wide, bordered by Sheila's chevrons and by Marty's fan-shaped patchworked corners. Francine laid her contribution around the medallion—tapered strips of green, and bands of yellow triangles shining inward towards the dolphins. As others added borders, the medallion grew to be a metre and a half across.

We presented the unfinished quilt top to Dory that winter when she hosted an evening of art, wine and music at her pottery studio in the old net loft at Cow Bay, then we began quilting in 1997, stitching swirls and starbursts of silver thread. Dolly embroidered puffed-cheeked wind faces with streaming hair, and Des added four beautiful sterling silver buttons to the quilt.

Sheila explained: "We express our feelings with fabric, threads, colour, texture, and with the gift of our time. Each of us held Dory in our hearts as we added strips, triangles, silver jewellery, all adding to the healing. It took us three years to complete the quilt. We first showed it to Dory when the quilt top was half-finished, and we feel that our quilt helped to sustain her in her recovery." Twenty-three years later, Dory wrote: "It was an overwhelming gift that I'm always grateful for and it represents my relief and safety when my breast cancer treatments ended. I would wrap myself up in it, and feel that I was part of a whole community, not just hanging out there on my own. Thankful that your thoughts and intentions were built into the warmth I could feel. And amazed at the wind, dolphin details, and the colours, and yes, Des's silver touch."

Smitten

I met Iain at a writers' group. The first evening, surrounded by strangers and clutching anxiously at the beginning pages of my how-to book, I was vividly aware of a very tall, very thin man with curling cornsilk hair. He seemed even more nervous than I was. He was reading aloud, his long legs twining around each other, then wrapping themselves around the legs of his chair. But his voice was deep and steady, and the story he read was witty and engaging. He looked up once, and I fell into his deep-pooled eyes, wanting to tangle my fingers in the rampant blond disorder of his hair. I was smitten.

Iain was the editor of the local paper, and we gradually got acquainted over the winter I lived in town. We trailed along when the writers' group adjourned to the bar, and I'd sit enthralled by the literary talk, and by the way our sidelong glances would suddenly collide. At the end of the evening, Iain would drive me to the group home door—I had to be in by midnight. We would kiss, bashfully circumspect, in the shadowy darkness beyond the lighted windows. I imagined cynical and worldly teenagers peering out and laughing, shocked at our slow, decorous courtship.

When winter and my live-in job ended, I moved back to Salt Lakes and we lost track of each other until the spring of 1986 when Iain bought Des's sailboat, *Mere Nime*, and sailed back into my life. Watching out the kitchen window, I would be thrilled to glimpse the white sail skimming across the harbour, the graceful shape tacking slowly nearer, gliding into the inlet where the sail was dropped in a chaotic flapping of fabric and a hectic twitching of ropes. I was touched that someone would go to such efforts just to see me.

I didn't yet understand that it was the romance and the lure of the sea itself that drew Iain, and that luckily, my little cabin and I myself embodied that romance for him. Iain and I embarked on exciting adventures in the sailboat. I had never sailed before and was not accustomed to boats that tipped on purpose. "Heeling," Iain called it, one of the many nautical terms he hoped I'd learn. The sailboat was very small; we cooked on a wee stove and slept on musty foamies in the bow, with the mast a vertical bundling board between us. Arlo went sailing too, a salty sea dog wearing a child's yellow raincoat.

I was introduced to sailing on Iain's tiny, graceful sailboat, *Mere Nime*. We went on exciting adventures voyaging in the waters beyond the harbour. Photo by Julie Moore.

We hiked in the muskeg meadows and along the rocky shores, went on picnics and beachcombing excursions in my yellow skiff, sidling up to floating logs or prying them off the high-tide shore and towing them back to my beach. We enjoyed beachcombing, but neither of us liked chainsawing much, so the logs accumulated on the beach and the woodshed stayed half-empty.

Iain still had an apartment in town, though he wasn't there much anymore. He was frustrated with his job at the newspaper and wanted to become a serious writer. He stayed at my cabin when I went to visit my family in early summer, and when I returned, he didn't leave. The next time I went away, I came back to find that he had built shelves in the front room, a settee that angled around the woodstove, and a desk in the corner for his typewriter and books. The cabin was *our* home now.

For a long time, we were shy with each other, not really at ease, probably not seeing each other very clearly. Iain saw me as self-reliant and independent, as a person who could take care of herself, who didn't need help. I saw him as a knight in shining raingear who would rescue me from my difficulties and dilemmas. "I like it that I don't have to take care of you," he said, though I was often mentally howling, "Oh, help me, change my life, take care of me," things I knew better than to say out loud.

He seemed impressed that I ran my own boat, and watched with admiration as I sharpened the chainsaw or checked the propane tank for

Arlo looks a bit forlorn wearing his raincoat, but he was a true sea dog and greatly enjoyed his nautical adventures. Maybe he was nervous because I was steering. Photo by Iain Lawrence.

leaks. I taught him the special clothesline knot that kept the skiff from slipping on the line. Through his eyes, I began to see that I was competent and capable, that I did indeed know how to take care of myself and had been doing so for some time.

Iain liked Salt Lakes and found the peculiarities of my life charming—the table made with old cast-iron sewing machine legs that held gallon jars of raisins and flour, the smoky kerosene lamps. He liked the wild riot of raspberries escaping the garden, and the old dog in the blue sweater. Rather than taking care of me, he took care of Arlo.

For several years, I had been dressing my old threadbare dog in castoff shrunken wool sweaters, until by now he looked naked without them. I'd slip a sweater over his head and stick his front feet through the armholes, roll the sleeves midway up his legs, then cut along the side seams with scissors. I'd wrap the front edges of the sweater around his back and tie them in a big tight knot. He was a natty, dapper, well-dressed dog, but truly ancient and decrepit.

Arlo's wiry terrier's pelt had lost its water-repellency, and he soaked up water like a sponge. When I patted his rump, his hind leg would spasmodically quiver and twitch, and he sometimes lost his footing in the boat and fell with a painful thump. The knot on his sweater made a good handle, and when he stumbled and fell as he ambled down the boardwalk, Iain would grab the sweater-knot to keep the poor dog upright.

Iain tenderly and matter-of-factly lifted Arlo in and out of the skiff, and carried him up and down the steep, low-tide dock ramps. When Arlo fell off the dock, Iain rescued him, jumping in after him if necessary. My nephews came to visit and crayoned invitations to Arlo's hundredth birthday party. Friends brought new sweaters, ribbon-wrapped bones and packages of hot dogs, and we had a wild party on the beach.

Iain's hair grew longer and his clothes shabbier; his ectomorphic physique was redefined in sinewy muscle. He had a knack for improvising peculiar structures that blended nicely with the cabin and the tumble-down sheds and outbuildings. He built a duck house out of old doors, but the first two ducklings disappeared shortly after moving in. Then Iain made a circus tent enclosure out of fishing nets, and we raised a couple of ducks to adolescence, only to find them one morning with their heads torn off, murdered by a marauding mink who didn't even eat them.

My job ended when the group home closed, and I decided on a sudden impulse to switch professions and go to aquaculture school. I was tired of loud, lippy, smart-alecky teenagers, and I thought, "fish don't talk." Three-quarters of a year later, I was a fish farmer, throwing food pellets into net pens, scrubbing tanks, dipping up fish, weighing fish, killing fish.

On April Fool's Day 1988, Iain quit work as a newspaper editor and became a fish farmer too. Arlo became a fish farm dog in his very old age, slowly pacing the net pens, eating the occasional pellet, and, of course, falling off the dock and being hauled out by his good friend Iain.

⁓❦

We sailed away in the summer of 1989 to explore the British Columbia coast in Iain's new boat, *Nid*. She was a small stout boat with brick-red sails and a tiny cabin, a miniature world filled with our dreams. Her name meant "nest" in French, and we were fledgling explorers venturing beyond the harbour, learning to fly on stormy seas. A triangular nest of foamies, blankets and scratchy wool sweaters filled the bow of the boat, and we snuggled close at night like birds in a high, wind-rocked tree, lulled into dense sea-drugged sleep.

We perched on top of the engine cover to cook, sat face-to-face eating dinner with our legs stretched across the narrow, precious floor space, feet resting on each other's benches while Arlo lay beneath our legs. We leaned precariously overboard to scrub our dishes in the salty waves. At night, we read sea stories aloud in the hazy kerosene glow of gimbaled brass lanterns.

I enjoyed working at the fish farm, being out on the water and using my muscles and my wits in ways that were new to me.

In rough weather, we made a nest for Arlo on the floor, packing him tightly with old blankets and duffel bags so he wouldn't bang his stiff knobby knees, or fall and upset his water dish. When he wasn't barricaded in this way, he sometimes lost control of his bowels, then slid helplessly in the mess as the boat rolled and plunged. We felt guilty for dragging him along on our voyage, except that he so obviously still loved the sea. On deck, he wore his raincoat over a thick sweater and stood stalwart, nose

Iain's new boat, *Nid*, took us on summer-long voyages down the coast. We stopped at Butedale, an abandoned cannery on the central coast of BC. Photo by Iain Lawrence.

to the wind that flattened his waterlogged hind end and revealed the shape of his noble skull. Iain kept one hand on the tiller and one hand on the dog.

I made a sling of brown canvas with wooden handles, like the log carriers advertised in magazines, and we used it to hoist the dog in and out of the dinghy. We called it Arlo's suitcase. Arlo looked very silly suspended above the water with legs dangling, tail hanging limp and forlorn from his suitcase. But he endured the contraption with grave composure, because he wanted to be on the beach.

Ashore, he stumbled gamely among the rocks, poked and sniffed through clumped seaweed looking for dead fish to roll in. A canine beach-comber, he sniffed out a pound of iridescent hamburger, plastic-wrapped on a Styrofoam raft. "He'll die happy," we joked as he nosed open the pack-age and ate the entire lump. But it didn't do him any harm.

We sailed back in the fall, into a new life on CBC Hill, where Hans and Margo had asked us to house-sit for nine months, a stay that would stretch into eleven years as caretakers. I liked the clean, warm house, prob-ably built in the 1960s but feeling modern after my long sojourn at Salt Lakes. There were light switches and a telephone and baseboard heaters, obliging hot water taps, and a stove that turned on and off with a dial. There was a fireplace, but we seldom lit it. We were tired of chopping wood.

Perched on the topmost knob of the hill, we lived within concentric circles. Our home was ringed by meadow, then by trees, then by a rumpled swath of harbour and the distant misty islands and mountains beyond. The

This aerial view of the CBC Hill tower, transmitter building and house shows both how isolated it seemed, and how close to town it actually was. Photo by Lonnie Wishart.

disk of meadow gleamed with long golden grasses, spiky ferns, the up-turned umbrellas of cow parsnip, and a scattered blaze of Scotch broom. The transmitter building and the tall orange and white radio tower centred the clearing, but I felt that everything radiated outward from us, from the house with its rectangle of emerald lawn.

We were alone, but not isolated. The lights of town could be seen beyond the trees, separated from us by the narrow harbour entrance. Dodge Cove's thirty houses were down a muddy path, and I could hike through the muskeg to Crippen Cove. Friends often climbed the hill to see us.

Our commute to work was complicated. We drove down the hill on "the tractor," a jaunty little all-terrain vehicle—a motorized kiddie-car for grown-ups. Iain held Arlo in the crook of one arm and steered with the other. I'd cling to him with Skipper, our new puppy, sandwiched between us. He would lift Arlo into a tangle of blankets in the skiff, then onto a foamy in the back of our VW van.

Iain and Skipper would take a big aluminum herring skiff out to the net-floats, but Arlo stayed in the van, parked outside the tank deck where I worked. At coffee breaks, I'd manoeuvre him out of the van and hold him upright for a few hobbling steps. We were lucky to have a boss who liked dogs. As it grew colder, we started leaving Arlo at home by the heater with disdainful Purrsilla, who would steal his dog food. We would come back to find Arlo lying in his own mess, distressingly tangled in pain, his gaunt ribs flailing. The vet said he had cancer.

Iain bought pork and a can of evaporated milk for Arlo's last meal, and we took our beloved old dog to the beach. It hurt to watch little Skipper hurling herself joyously across the sand while Arlo's spindly flanks trembled and gave way beneath him. We were quiet on the trip to town. At the vet's, I cradled Arlo on the cold, high table as he was injected, then held him until his breath slowed and deepened and stopped.

CBC Hill and Dodge Cove

Our first morning in the house on CBC Hill, we awoke to a horrendous lightning storm. I was terrified because we were right under the tall radio tower, which I imagined attracting fiery thunderbolts. We were late for work because I was too scared to leave the house.

In our clean, bright, spacious new home, our belongings looked bedraggled and worn out, and they smelled. Everything we brought from Salt Lakes, especially our books and clothes, had a brash fungoidal taint, a hint of mouse droppings and decay. I was suddenly aware that anything we had taken on our boat trips reeked of mildew and diesel fumes, though I hadn't noticed this while aboard.

But our new home had its own peculiarities: a huge brass ship's bell on the front porch that chimed dolefully when the wind blew, and small acid-green frogs and high-jumping cricket-spiders that lived in the basement, most likely in the cistern that held our water supply. When it rained, our living room filled with the soothing and meditative gurgle of rainwater funnelling from the eavestroughs through a filter made of old nylon stockings and into the cavernous concrete vault directly below the sofa. White worms grew through the nylon if we neglected to change the stockings regularly. Turning a tap or flushing the toilet activated a whining electric pump which urged the water upward.

Our front yard was magical in the spring, with a meadow full of yellow daffodils, and the entrance to the harbour and the distant islands beyond.

Our springtime view out the front window was stunning, a field of daffodils with the harbour entrance and the misty islands beyond. We had electricity at last, so we bought a computer, then vied with each other for its use. Iain worked seriously on his writing, and I was anxious to finish my "design-as-you-sew" quilt book. I was frequently enraged by the computer and by my own ineptitude. Gone were the placid days of pen and paper and kerosene lamps; I had rejoined the

The CBC radio tower is on the left, our new home is on the right, with the transmitter building behind it. Photo by Garry Sattich.

twentieth century and was racing full-tilt to catch up with the age of computers.

The wooden-planked helicopter pad that perched on the edge of the lawn like a banished patio was used when the CBC technicians came to tend the transmitter equipment. Arrivals were always unexpected, heralded by a rackety, accelerating din as the helicopter swooped over the hill and hovered above the house. As it settled downward in a ferocious whirring clatter, a spiraling wind would flatten the grass and flowers. The dancers on Iain's whirligig would suddenly quick-step a frantic tango to the repeated banging of the screen door as the radio technicians exited the helicopter in a careful crouch.

I'd peer around the corner from the hallway, waiting for the machine to miss the platform, for the huge propeller to fly off and slice through the house like an avenging Ninja star. "There's only one bolt holding that thing on," Iain always said as the silver blades whizzed past our picture window. "The pilots call it the Jesus bolt." The departure of the helicopter would leave a dull void, and I'd listlessly make Jello or clean the sewing machine.

The houses, shacks and boat sheds of Dodge Cove dangled like colourful plastic charms from a bracelet of gravel that circled a rumpled taffeta bay. I'd gaze out the kitchen window through winter dusk towards the scattered sequins of light in the village below. Scraps of sound drifted upwards—a thudding axe, the shrill voices of children disembarking from the school

Dodge Cove was a small, well-established community with homes and gardens along a gravel path, and large boat sheds on pilings at the shore.

Dodge Cove kids soon learned to row. Parents insisted on tightly zipped lifejackets at all times and kept a vigilant eye on the young voyagers as they explored the cove. Photo by Garry Sattich.

ferry, the barking of dogs. Red pinpricks of light moved swiftly towards the dock as commuter boats returned home. A larger fishboat slid in slowly with a quiet, steadfast throb.

Up on the hill, I was distant from Dodge Cove's family-oriented bustle. I was not part of the boating "carpools" for hockey practice and ballet lessons in town, or of the child-minding network that allowed kids to roam freely from one end of the village to the other or to row a boat within the safety of the cove. I sometimes attended a birthday party or the Easter potluck, but my favourite celebration was the winter solstice, when children and adults gathered on the cold dark shore of Marine Bay and launched home-made candle boats into the midnight waves.

I joined the women in an empty house in the village, where they had set up a quilting frame to work on Joline's baby quilt. She wasn't a baby anymore—she was almost two—but the pass-the-medallion quilt had expanded border by border to twin-bed size. It was now considered a gift for the whole family. Whenever they had time, the women gathered informally to stitch, as they wanted to finish the quilt before Joline and her parents returned from a trip. When the quilt was done, the women just left it on the family's couch. As Francine explained, "that way, they can take their time to look at it, and cry if they want to."

Francine had been startled by the informality of our quilt-making when she first joined us. "You're suffering from culture shock," we'd tease her when

Jane came to visit with her daughters Kate and Nora and their friend Joline, and they tried on patchwork bonnets I had made.

she worried over exact dimensions or asked what the colour scheme was. She had learned to quilt with the Oona River quilters, famous on the north coast for their stunning group-made quilts which were carefully planned and meticulously sewn, with lavishly hand-embroidered scenes and tiny quilting stitches. "I was very shocked by the quilting when I came to Dodge Cove," Francine told us. "To me, quilting had to be seven stitches to the inch with quilting thread. I was amazed to see that you can use embroidery thread, any colour, any stitch. Now I like the acceptance here—it relaxes me not to worry if my work is good enough. And I like the diplomacy between people, nobody wanting to hurt anyone by being critical." But she was still frustrated at times, and exclaimed about her struggles with a difficult fabric: "That fabric—it raised a commotion when I tried to sew it down!"

Lou, who also learned to quilt at Oona River, had been similarly shocked by our casual approach to quilt-making when she joined us. Yet she later wrote a glowing tribute to our collective creativity:

> The thing that struck me most when I first started quilting with these women was their panache, their zestful confidence that what they made would be beautiful. They didn't plan quilts, they just made them, and they were warm and welcoming to anyone who wanted to join them.
>
> They never said: "The corners don't meet," but always "Isn't that purple gorgeous next to that batik?" And that is characteristic of these quilters: a love for rich vibrant colours and textures, silks and satins, brocades and velvets, batiks and prints with pictures of birds, fish, and butterflies. Perhaps it's the long grey days of winter, the somberness of the rain and fog, and the pervasive green of the woods and waters of this coast that make them respond so wholeheartedly to red, purple, and flame-gold.

We used the helicopter pad to lay out the squares for Kim's quilt. Ginger, Kristin, Francine and Carmel are pondering the placement of the squares. Photo by Carol Manning.

Now, I've contributed to four quilts, and "they" has become "we." My life feels richer for the creativity, friendship, and love of the shared endeavour, the whole that is more than the sum of its parts. This group is as warm and loving as the quilts we make, gifts from the heart and hands.

The helicopter pad in front of our house was a spacious outdoor workspace, and the quilters came up the hill to arrange the squares for Kim's quilt in the blessed sunshine. We were making a comfort quilt for our friend who was enduring cancer treatments. It looked like a giant board game as one woman put down a square and someone else picked it up and moved it, saying, "No, it clashes there. Let's try it here." Then other hands reached out and rearranged the squares again. "The flowers are upside-down," and "Too many blues next to each other." The women joked and laughed when the wind fluttered the orange tarp they were kneeling on, but there was a sad and hurried undertone to the day. Nobody wanted to say it, but we all hoped our friend would still be alive when the quilt was finished.

Sheila remembers that "it was one of the saddest quilts I ever worked on, because of the uncertainty about her illness." Jane recalls, "I was new to the quilting group and Kim's quilt was very moving for me to be involved with. It seemed very sisterly and supportive to be making a quilt for her

Ginger, Carmel, Francine and Kristin are on the helicopter pad trying to reach consensus on arranging the squares for Kim's quilt. Photo by Carol Manning.

We photographed Kim's quilt and the quilters on the Dodge Cove dock. Kim stands on the right beside her quilt. Photo by Karen McKinster.

when she was going through such a hard time." Lorrie sent a square from Vancouver embroidered with a circle of people holding hands to symbolize a community of love and concern. Sheila, whose quilt square was an exuberant star pulsating with energy, says, "we all saw the optimism and courage that Kim had and we tried to feel it ourselves and to reflect it in the quilt."

Dolly's square was an appliquéd sunset. She said, "each person put emotion into their square. Mine was calm and peaceful to look at, because Kim needed to be very calm and relaxed, she needed quiet time. And Marie's square, with the cartoon pelican in a hammock, has a sense of fun that was needed as well." There were several pelican squares, because Kim and her partner lived aboard a boat named *Rupert Pelican*. Ten-year old Auriane made a bright yellow star dotted with French knots, and seven-year-old Elize made a smiley-faced moon embellished with beads. But the little girl mislaid her square and it wasn't included in the quilt. When she found it months later, she made a pillow for Kim.

It took all morning to decide on the placement of the squares and another hour to choose the sashing fabric. We were grateful for Francine's quick precision as she calculated the dimensions of the sashing strips in French, then supervised the cutting in English. Some of the squares were too small, so at the last minute we were adding little strips. It took the rest of the day and three sewing machines stitching at once to get the quilt top together, and there was no time left to finish it. The quilt went down the hill with the women and was taken from house to house to be quilted and bound.

When we gave the quilt to Kim at a party on International Women's Day in 1992, she shocked us by joking, "gee, you don't need to have a baby to get a quilt—you can have cancer instead." She was wan and emaciated from radiation, but grinning invincibly. Later, Kim reflected, "I'd already felt the warmth and concern for me, and I was just amazed when it was manifested in a quilt. The warmth and caring was enough, but on top of it, I got a quilt." Five years later, Kim joined us on quilting day to stitch love and caring into a quilt for another friend fighting cancer.

The Quilting Amoebae

Our quilting circle was nameless until 1992, when we labelled ourselves the Coastal Quilters for the quilt show at the museum. But Carol called us the Quilting Amoebae, seeing us as a colourful, amorphous entity that absorbed anyone who wanted to stitch on a quilt.

The quilting amoebae engulfed Carol in 1985, and she's worked on many of our community-made quilts since. She described her first quilt gathering as a journey out of isolation. She was a teacher who had just moved to Crippen Cove after living many years in town. She seldom saw her colleagues after work because she was boating back to the cove, and she missed out on island potlucks and beach gatherings since she had to be at work.

"I was isolated and alone, living a reclusive life, and separated from activities in both parts of my life," she told me. "I was invited to an evening of quilting at Dodge Cove. I wanted to go and knew I needed to go. I had to rise above my insecurities, put on a façade of confidence. I checked the tide table so I wouldn't get caught on the mud flats, and set out on my own. I don't remember tying up my skiff or walking up the path. I only remember sitting at Sheila's kitchen table when Wendy came in the door. The quilts were for her twin girls. Becoming part of this group was significant and therapeutic, linking me emotionally with a community, and fulfilling some of the roles of an extended family."

From Carol Manning's poem/memoir, "Into the Void":

Then the quilters,
working together to honour life's events:
the arrivals, the departures, and the messiness in between.
The quilters, my Sisters of Mercy, my lifeline when all was in flux,
who tended my uncertainties,
who encouraged my expression.
An amoebic group with far reaching pseudopods
enclosing a changing collection of people.
Unexpected, casual friendships evolved into
a caring, accepting, fluid community.

Carol moved to Dodge Cove and continued commuting to town. She was one of the few people who didn't complain about the short winter days and the long, dark nights. "I like the dark," she commented. When we made her a quilt, my square depicted Carol coming home on a winter night. Her appliquéd skiff passes the ruby bead of the red can-buoy, leaving a rippling, silver-threaded vee in the black water as it heads for the glitter of the village lights.

The quilt square I made for Carol's quilt depicts her heading home in the dark, with the ruby light of the marker buoy to guide her way, and the lights of Dodge Cove glimmering in the distance.

Finn's quilt was not a secret from Marty, his mother. She had attended a quilting day where we arranged oceanic motifs into a fantastical undersea tableau. We had dozens of cut-out fabric fish, along with crabs and other sea critters. Marty's mom had sent us a big, beautifully embroidered fish, and Sheila had printed an exact replica of a spiny rockfish onto fabric by inking up a frozen fish and pressing it onto cloth.

We started out trying to create a realistic scene, but as Marty commented, "I still clearly remember the moment when Sheila started overlapping fish randomly here and there, and how novel and freeing that felt, and how the group instantly adopted that idea." Her poem captures the day.

"Finn's Quilt," by Marty Sutmoller
– *for Karen*

They climbed up CBC hill carrying food
and fabric fish to arrange on a quilt top.
An excuse to ignore longline repairs,
for red wine, friends, and forgetting.

Fish surfaced from scrap bins:
Brandon's batik puffer shirt, pointed angels, rainbow parrots,

some cast-offs from the wild, Wilde-Fish quilt
constructed five years earlier, hauled out and overhauled.
Loose talk drifted to men while Jane happily gutted
a vintage embroidered couch-cushion.
Lopping off its avocado edges (she was never fond of that colour anyway),
the spilled innards tossed for a clean start.

By glass two, Francine had dismembered rows of frayed bobbles
once hand-tied by great-grandma, repurposed in a heap.
Wee scraps cinched-in-the-round, like seine nets, or
washed-up beach floats trailing bedraggled seaweed.

Sheila dredged a real halibut from her deep freeze,
thawed just enough to press its fin filigree in gold paint.
Too, a purple snapper gasping with blown-out eyes,
heaved-up on some line, its shocked expression frozen still.

Fabric extras were trolled from Kristin's stash.
The primo catch-of-the-day being a sandy, stretch-polyester strip
from her Salt Lake bell-bottom swinger-days,
sewn down off-kilter as a rumpled sea-floor.

By the bottom of the second glass, amid trials
of persnickety (Kristin's word) fish placement,
a slurry idea arose from the Ray Troll fans
to jam fish willy-nilly into one roiling mass of gill and tail.

And so, like a fish feeding, we entwine tidal carnage,
hand-tuck Thai silk seagrass, starfish, and shells, over and under
swimmers to anchor gumboot chitons, and permanently hook
that tipsy moment onto a mottled tie-dyed blue.

This gift crafted before being plunged
back to a fisher's life of skate-sets,
bucking the three-metre swells beyond Kiusta,
bearing hard and wet, the full force of an incoming season.

Marty dedicated the poem to Karen, the most experienced fish-
ing-woman in our quilting circle.

⁓⊹

Lou hosted an idyllic quilt gathering in the spring of 1995, inviting the quilters to her home on an island beyond the harbour. It was a grand adventure for the women to travel so far in their small boats, to wheelbarrow their quilts and potluck offerings up a long boardwalk to the estuary where Lou's floathouse was beached, and to spend several days visiting and quilting outside in the golden sunlight or inside in lantern glow.

An array of fish swim through the seaweed on Finn's quilt. We had a riotous time arranging and rearranging this scene.

The quilting amoebae frequently took over the Dodge Cove schoolhouse, a long, low building with big windows and a motley collection of wooden benches and vintage silver-legged kitchen tables. No longer used as a school, it had become the community gathering place for potlucks, work bees, play days, meetings, and dances.

I remember a prodigious quilting day, when the schoolhouse was drenched in colour as we worked together on seven group-made quilts. The quilt for Norah was stretched out on the floor, purple and turquoise with giant appliquéd elephants in the four corners. Emily's baby quilt hung on the wall behind it. A quiet semi-circle of heads bent over embroidery hoops in the far corner as Dolly demonstrated 3-D Brazilian embroidery. A group of women knelt on the floor, laying out a pattern for Rowena's goodbye quilt. The squares for Carol's quilt and for Dolly's quilt were piled on a bench next to the table where our get-well quilt for Dory was being quilted.

Finn's undersea quilt was almost finished. We were adding seaweed, skeins of tiny "yo-yos"

Quilting outdoors was a pleasure when we visited Lou in the outer islands. Lou and Sheila are stitching, while Marie looks on.

Lou hosted a memorable quilt retreat at her floathouse on the quiet estuary of an island beyond the harbour. We quilted, feasted, and explored the forest and shore.

that Colleen had given us. Her great-grandmother had made these oddly appealing decorations for a pillowcase by gathering small circles of fabric into little puckered disks and sewing them together in rows.

Colleen had shown me the matching yo-yo coverlet, taking me up the steep wooden stairs of her cottage to a room under the eaves with a carved wooden bedstead covered in hundreds of small, glowing circles of colour. "Want to see something else?" she asked, kneeling to reach under the bed. She rolled out a creamy shaft about two metres long, burnished like old silk and gnarled with spiral markings. "It's a narwhale tusk. Hunters gave it to us when we lived in the Arctic," she said, rolling it gently back under the bed.

Francine brought lace from Osland, an abandoned cannery village at the mouth of the Skeena River, where she had lived years before with her partner and baby. Exploring an old building in the tiny Scandinavian ghost town, she had found a bonanza of lace in the warped drawer of an old treadle sewing machine. Finely knitted and crocheted strips, squares, triangles, and a dumbbell of ancient yellowing lace. They were beautiful but odd, especially the dumbbell. We could imagine no purpose for this yard-long strip of lace with intricate bulbous ovals at either end.

The big lacy saw-tooth piece shaped like the scaffold in a game of hangman was probably unfinished, perhaps meant to frame a window or

Dolly, Sheila S., Wendy, Maria and Jane are busy stitching on a quilting day at the former Dodge Cove schoolhouse, now a community gathering place. Photo by Lonnie Wishart.

edge a tablecloth. The crocheted vee may have been made to adorn a modest décolleté. But the giant triangles? The dumbbell?

"Cabin fever," someone said. "She went crazy and just kept knitting." We laughed in uneasy solidarity with the unknown woman. We could picture her knitting witlessly in a stark cold house with sagging floors, staring out through lacy curtains at the hostile rain.

We knew it could drive you crazy to live on the north coast if you didn't want to be there, and sometimes even if you did. Or drive you to desperation like the young woman we knew who hiked into the forest behind Dodge Cove with a gun and didn't come back; like the fisherman who wrapped himself in heavy boom-chains and went overboard to fix the bottom of his boat. Cabin fever. Bushed.

I could imagine the Swedish lady in long-ago Osland, pale hair tightly bound, her deftly moving fingers clenched tight on silver needles. Pale blue eyes staring out at the endless flowing river and the sombre trees, the rain at dusk, or blowing sleet. Waiting, knitting, worrying about the baby's earache, about money and the leaky roof and mildewed pillows, the mouldy cheese. Crocheting numbly, wondering when her husband would come back from the sea or the mountains; wondering what she would do if he did not.

But perhaps I have her wrong. She may have been merry and laughing, eager to throw off the constraints of the old country and to lead a

Sheila D., Maria and Sheila S. are enjoying a laugh as they stitch on Dolly's quilt.
Photo by Lonnie Wishart.

broader, freer life in the Canadian wilderness. She may have lost herself in the swoop of gulls, practised dancing on the wharf, gazed exultant as shivering splinters of moonlight traced wrinkled zig-zags on the waves. Perhaps she hiked the muskeg in brave suspendered trousers, wrote poems, went fishing. Perhaps she sat crocheting on a rock, pondering the low-tide shores and counting her blessings.

I can only imagine her. But whether she was a timid stay-at-home or bold adventuress, her concerns and pursuits seemed familiar, understandable, quite similar to ours. Her shadowy presence at our quilting day enlarged our circle, bestowed on us an eccentric creativity, and linked us to the north coast past. If she could have truly joined us, I wondered if she would have laughed or cried to see us trying to fit her crocheted dumbbell into Marty's baby's quilt.

Hanging Our Quilts on Gallery Walls

My friends were skeptical when I suggested displaying our group-made quilts at the little art gallery in the old Museum of Northern BC in Prince Rupert. "Exhibit our quilts? Why would we want to do that?" they wondered. They valued the quilts as meaningful communal gifts, but had never considered them as works of art. To humour me, they agreed to have a quilt show at the museum in October 1992.

We borrowed back twenty-four quilts that had been made and given as gifts in the previous decade, and counted up the number of folks who had participated. Thirty-six women, eight men, and four children. Most of the quilts had been made in the north, with four made in Vancouver. We were overwhelmed as we unwrapped quilt after quilt after quilt. Not one of us had ever seen all the quilts before; I had never even seen some of the quilts made at Crippen Cove. The four Vancouver quilts fascinated us with their quirky verve and flair.

On the pristine white walls of the gallery, the quilts glowed in the spotlights, their colours newly vivid. We felt proud of our collective creativity, but also shy and abashed by the sudden public focus on our quilts, which had been made as very personal expressions of community and friendship. The quilts had been made as gifts, with no pretensions of being

Olivier's quilt, made by the Vancouver quilters, amused and amazed us with its sophisticated and quirky squares. Photo by Carmel Pepin.

The art gallery at the Museum of Northern BC glowed with vibrant colour. Kristin's quilt (my quilt!) is on a quilting frame, with quilts for Claire, Siobhan, Mia and Maxim on the wall behind. Photo by Carmel Pepin.

art, but were being admired by strangers in an art gallery. Lorrie and Anneke came north to videotape the exhibit and to interview the northern quilters, who were bemused by all the attention. "I'll be glad when this is over and we can get back to quilt-making," one commented.

We had spent the afternoon hanging the quilts and the early evening setting up the table of wine and snacks for the opening night party. Just before the festivities began, Ginger took me outside for a smoke. When we returned fifteen minutes later, there was a gorgeous big quilt that I had never seen before, stretched out on a quilting frame in the middle of the gallery. Everyone was looking at me and smiling and clapping. The quilt was for me!

A placard beside it read:

> This quilt has come from a wish to celebrate Kristin's creativity and friendship. Much of the inspiration in our community quilts has come from Kristin's own quilting example. She has so often reassured us that what we put together in colour, texture, and shapes do work, though they may rarely be perfect in traditional quilting form.
>
> She has helped us to see that our combined effort creates a successful whole beauty. Her perspective and encouragement has found us doing more together and on our own.

The Coastal Quilters of the north coast and those who now live in the lower mainland all thought, simultaneously it seemed, that it was time to acknowledge Kristin's quilting energy. We have done so with this quilt.

I could hardly see the quilt through my tears. I was stunned by the unexpectedness of such a grand gift. The room seemed filled with strong, loving feelings and with great gaiety and giddiness. I was in a daze, so excited and surprised that I could hardly focus on the details of the quilt, or on the beaming faces surrounding me. I suddenly understood why my quilting friends had seemed so distant and aloof in the weeks past. They had been secretly working on my quilt, with the tight deadline of opening night of the quilt exhibit. They had created this intricate gift in great secrecy, in a very short time. Although the quilt was on the quilting frame, I felt wrapped in its warmth, and in the wonderful friendships that it represented.

I learned that friends who had moved to Vancouver had made the large centre medallion. Lorrie started it off with a star, and others added borders concentrically in pass-the-medallion fashion. Shelley and Bill cut up her grandmother's embroidered linens to use in their border, and Linda sculpted 3-D fabric hands plying needle and thread.

Margo's borders joined blue and red fabrics with seams that undulated in elegant curves, following a pattern that Hans had drafted. Margo later explained, "he plotted the line on his computer and we printed it out. I cut the pieces out and we figured out how to sew them. I wanted to give something to Kristin that maybe she hadn't quite done before. From what she said when she got the quilt, she was wondering how we had done that wavy line, which was very pleasing to me." Indeed, I was impressed with the precision of the deeply curved seams.

Meanwhile, my northern friends were each making their own small medallion squares. The large Vancouver medallion was mailed north, and the quilters in Dodge Cove devised a layout of individual medallions surrounding the elaborate central panel, with yellow lattice strips uniting the whole. This quilt was a grand reminder of what I already knew, that my coastal friends were generous and warm; creative, industrious, and colourful; and I was lucky to have them in my life.

As locals and tourists visited the quilt show, the quilters felt an increasing pride and self-awareness of the aesthetic value of the quilts. Mary Bywater Cross, a tourist on her way to Alaska, viewed the exhibit and wrote in the guestbook: "This is a very special and unique exhibit of quilts and their makers. It conveys so much about your lives, your dreams, and your interdependence as women striving to survive today. It's a pure example of

Lorrie placed a star in the centre of the quilt made for me, and Linda crafted a 3-D hand holding a needle and "stitching" around the star. Photo by Carol Manning.

regional quiltmaking free of commercial influences from outside. The style, the fabrics, the need to make quilts; it's what quilting is all about."

Ms. Cross phoned me later, and I learned that she was a quilt historian. She was quite excited to have "discovered" us, and she asked me to write a research paper about our quilts and our communities for the American Quilt Study Group (AQSG). I agreed, though I scarcely knew how to go about this task. My friends were surprised that we needed to be discovered, but pleased by her interest. They agreed to answer my questions as I "researched" their marine-based lifestyles, their friendships and interconnections, and their apparently unique methods of quilt-making.

I made up surveys, interviewed my friends, and wrote up as scholarly a piece as I could manage. My paper was accepted for publication and for presentation at the annual AQSG seminar. The title was quite a mouthful: "Out of the Mainstream: Innovative Group Quiltmaking in an Isolated Coastal Community in Northern British Columbia, Canada." My friends were rather amused but also very proud of me, of themselves, and of our quilts.

The introduction to my paper read:

The distinctive quilts made cooperatively by a group of women living on an island in coastal British Columbia offer a fresh perspective on the development of the art form. An inventive, resourceful, and non-dogmatic approach to quiltmaking reflects the demands of the quilters' rugged lifestyle and the qualities valued in their close-knit communities. In fourteen years, they've made twenty-eight quilts together, with little input from conventional quilting sources. Their elegantly eccentric quilts feature three-dimensional embellishments, non-conventional fabric sources, spontaneous free-form quilting, and embroidery stitched through all three layers of the quilt.

The author surveyed the quilters to pinpoint how they learned to quilt, the influences that affected them, their sources of inspiration, and their methods of working together. Lifestyle, isolation, and the lack of outside influences are related to the emergence of a regional style; and common island traits (cooperation, independence, resourcefulness, and frugality) are linked to the quiltmaking process. Quotations from the quilters help answer the question: Why do women make quilts together?

I travelled back to Maine for the seminar and gave my slideshow presentation to great applause. I had misunderstood the guidelines for slides, not realizing that only a dozen or so were needed. I flashed through more than a hundred slides during my ten-minute talk, dazzling the scholarly audience with glimpses of our quilts, our suddenly picturesque homes on tree-clad northern shores, our quilting days, our gardens, kids and boats.

Later, I stood waiting to display the quilt my friends had given me. The walls of the hall were bedecked with masterpiece New England quilts, all with modulated colours, perfect piecing, and tiny quilting stitches. I stared at the big mis-matched stitches that

The centre of my quilt was made by former northerners who had moved to Vancouver. Margo, Lorrie, and Anneke are holding the quilt top, while the kids pose beneath.

I was filled with pride and trepidation when I presented the quilt made for me at the American Quilt Study Group Seminar in Portland, Maine, in 1993.

showed through the back of my quilt. I was embarrassed by the smell of the quilt itself, with its lingering odor of woodsmoke and north coast mustiness. Then, two white-gloved ladies unfurled my brilliantly coloured quilt amid the delighted clapping of the audience, and I felt very proud of my own masterpiece quilt and of the women who had made it.

Visiting Vancouver

On my trips to Seattle to see my family, I usually tried to squeeze in a stop in Vancouver to visit my now citified ex-northern friends. The tight bonds that had held our harbour community together had loosened in Vancouver, but the transplanted northerners still got together occasionally. Two ongoing rituals seemed especially cohesive—quilting together, and going out for a beer after the yoga class that many attended. I joined them for the beer and the quilting, for parties, and meals at exotic ethnic restaurants. And as I had at Salt Lakes, I went from house to house to visit my three special friends.

Gabriel's lilac bush was blooming in a big Chinese pot by Lorrie's front door. She welcomed me with a hug and introduced me to her son Ezra, born since the last time I had seen her. Wearing little Ezra in a backpack, she washed dishes while we visited, stepping deftly over the toys on

Kathy, Anneke and Shelley enjoy the friendship and creativity of a Vancouver quilting day as they stitch on Nicou's quilt.

the floor. She seemed tired and subdued, resigned to the rigors of motherhood. She was about to embark on life as a single mom and seemed weighed down with responsibility. But her warm sociability was undiminished, and we caught up on each other's lives as she cooked supper.

Lorrie was planning to move into Anneke's house, but she daydreamed about returning north again. Many of my Vancouver friends shared a similar ambivalence, a similar nostalgia for the north coast. Most of the women's lives seemed harder to me, more rigorous in the big city, their options more limited.

Lorrie was the ringleader for the Vancouver quilters, who had by now worked together on nine group-made quilts. Their quilting circle enlarged as city friends joined in. Lorrie also taught a quilting class at the local community centre, but found that the carefree, inclusive, communal creativity we had always taken for granted didn't transfer easily.

Nine-year-old Elisha set an impeccable table in the kitchen nook with a brilliant batik tablecloth, napkins carefully rolled in holders she had made, bagels in a brightly glazed, handmade pottery bowl. She showed me a shelf in the china cupboard with her pottery creations—an open-ended curl of clay for serving cheese, a flat slab for sushi, a round-faced "sweet girl" sugar bowl with a hat for a lid. Her craft table was under the windows in the narrow sunporch/bathroom upstairs. Papier mâché dried on the back porch, and her boldly stitched embroidery and quilt squares filled a basket in the dining room.

After the meal, Elisha balanced gracefully on a sturdy chest to practise a song that Lorrie's friend Holly was teaching her. "The coho flash silver all over the bay," she sang, gazing intently at Ezra as though to mesmerize him, tapping her tambourine with precision. Ezra chortled and scooted along the floor, shaking a string of blue ceramic beads.

When I went back to Vancouver three months later, Lorrie and Linda picked me up at the airport. Ezra was walking, and Lorrie's sparkle and gaiety had returned. She seemed happy. We sat at Lorrie's old kitchen table with its familiar cross-stitched gingham tablecloth, eating toast in her new home upstairs at Anneke's house. Ezra, wearing tiny black gumboots, was alternately grave and merry as he played peekaboo and a fall-on-the-floor game of his own devising.

⁓✿

Linda's neighbourhood was a mix of light industrial and urban sleaze, with the dubious glamour of prostitutes parading on the street corners and movie crews filming chase scenes in the alleys or on the flat roofs of nearby buildings. They sometimes commandeered the shabbily picturesque back stairs and wooden porches of her apartment building, moving Linda's pot-ted plants without asking, and setting up a folding director's chair outside her kitchen window.

I buzzed the ancient intercom, obeyed the hand-printed notice to "Be Sure the Door Is Shut!" and lugged my suitcase up three flights of shiny, well-scrubbed stairs to the warm oasis of Linda's apartment. Her frugal ingenuity that I remembered so well from Salt Lakes was evident here too. She had made an elegant, Japanese-style lamp using thin cedar slats unravelled from a rummage sale window blind. An old luggage cart hung over the stove to store pots and pans. The guest bed was a quite functional arrangement of planks that could be dismantled or folded into a narrow couch. She saved her compost in an ice cream bucket and biked it over to Lorrie's garden.

Linda was excited about her new job of collecting otoliths, the tiny ear-bones of freshly caught halibut, then scrutinizing them under a microscope to determine the age of the fish. She said she had worn out her thumbs at her old job counting salmon, which involved picking up each heavy fish and incessantly clicking the tally device.

As I walked up the steps, Margo came around the corner of the house with a laundry basket. She was serenely harried, on a tight schedule, swabbing the kitchen counter as she answered an endless series of phone calls, part of her job as supervisor of fish-monitoring personnel. She had been working overtime, and this brief time off was filled with housework and family responsibilities. A son was home sick, the dishwasher needed loading, her desk was piled high with paperwork.

Margo had no regrets about moving to Vancouver because of the good schooling and other opportunities available for the kids. They rented a well-kept older house on a tree-lined street. Margo still connected with her old friends and had made new friends, but felt that she didn't have a real community in the city like the one she had left up north.

I asked Galen, now eleven, about city life versus north coast life. He answered thoughtfully: "We were a lot more independent at Dodge Cove. We didn't have to worry about strangers, kidnappers, all that stuff they teach you about here in Vancouver. In Dodge Cove you could ride your bike around, do whatever you wanted. A lot of people might say it was dangerous, riding boats and stuff, but when you are raised there and grow up in boats, you didn't really think like that. And the kids there were all close friends."

The Vancouver quilters looked as though they were all in bed together. The luxuriant satin bulk of Linda's quilt rested on a low coffee table and spread buoyantly over the women's laps. Without a quilting frame to control it, the

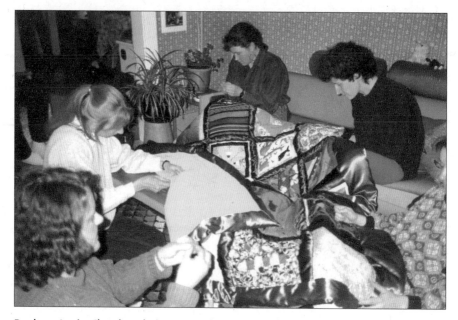

Daphne, Annie, Cheryl, and Nicou are engulfed in a puffy expanse of colour as they stitch diligently through the thick layers of Linda's quilt.

quilt gently rippled and undulated as Anneke interviewed and videotaped the quilters while they stitched. After videotaping the quilt show at the museum, Anneke had decided to document the quilters both north and south. The women chatted unselfconsciously as they sewed, for Anneke was their friend, and this was a sociable occasion.

Linda had already been ceremoniously presented with a stack of quilt squares on her fortieth birthday. Many months later, the squares had been united with a lattice of green satin, and the quilt top had been basted over three thick layers of batting. The camera caught Linda's reactions on seeing the quilt. "It's great! It's huge! And I'm thrilled," she exclaimed. "Receiving a quilt is wonderful, really neat. All your friends quilting together for you and thinking about it, planning it out, and picking out special things that you might like. I can hardly wait until it's finished."

Ghislaine commented: "What I really like is how the person who gets the quilt can read through the quilt and see who has done what, and laugh at some of the jokes in the quilt, and some of the things people put in because they have special rapport with the person that receives the quilt." Many of the squares express this rapport. Linda's friend Larry's square was a picture of Bubalina, the dog they both loved. Young Elisha's square was a crayoned drawing of a winged woman with a sceptre, and the words, "Linda, my fairy godmother." Cecile's square celebrated Linda's fishing experience with a 3-D gillnet of tulle encircling a school of fancy fish.

Mountains, ocean and trees are the backdrop of a grand quilting day up on CBC Hill. The women are stitching on two quilts stretched out on the grass—Linda's quilt and the quilt I was given. Photo by Linda Gibbs.

Daphne spoke of the process of working with friends to create Linda's quilt: "What I think of is the evolution of all the pieces spread out on the floor the first night. Everything looked real plain. It evolved over time as we all got together to work on it. It changed. What I like most is the community feeling of people coming together, because it changes your own ideas of what you are doing."

Linda pointed to a square with two lively looking, appliquéd feet: "Those are my feet!" Anne explained, "I remember watching Linda dance with such joy and vigor. If there is music, it is rare to see Linda not dancing. So the dancing feet are my contribution to her quilt. The feet have a lovely pattern of flowers which suggests bright-patterned stockings, spring, growth, life in the dance."

Linda's quilt was the first one that Anne worked on, and she was quite reflective about the process: "What struck me was the celebration of each other's lives. The giving of time and care in the making—a loving act, and the ability of people to come together and to make creative decisions together. Also, the idea that the quilt gives warmth, protects—what a gift. And the creative act of bringing the many, many pieces of the puzzle into a whole, a perfect symbol of the coming together of the group."

When I had a brief lay-over at the Vancouver airport, Lorrie and Linda met me by the luggage carousel, bringing Linda's quilt to show me. I had

Linda and I are showing off her quilt on the dock at Cow Bay. The appliquéd feet in the centre of the quilt were made by Annie to celebrate Linda's love of dancing.

taken my quilt to Seattle to show my mom, so I pulled it out of my suitcase and we spread each quilt out over a row of baggage carts, watched by curious travellers. Since both quilts could use more quilting, we decided to trade quilts for a while, so friends in the north could quilt on the southern quilt, and vice versa. Linda planned to visit me a few weeks later, so she would bring my quilt back, and retrieve her own. As my flight was called, Linda quickly folded up my quilt while Lorrie and I struggled to get Linda's thick puffy quilt into my small suitcase, and then we hugged goodbye.

The Dodge Cove women spent an evening at Jane's stitching on Linda's quilt, marvelling that the Vancouver women had had the patience to sew through three dense layers of batting. During Linda's visit, we had a quilting day outside in the sun on CBC Hill, with the women of Dodge Cove and Crippen Cove working on both our quilts. It felt as though our stitches connected friends north and south.

We Gather Together

The sky was clear, the earth frozen. I walked slowly down the back path through the woods in bright daylight, over dry boards and frozen puddles. Tight buds were forming on the huckleberry bushes but the early spring foliage was sparse. I was going down the path to Dodge Cove for fun, for a party on International Women's Day, and I had time to look about.

On too many early mornings I had dashed down the narrow winding trail, hurtling through the winter darkness with my flashlight growing dim as I raced to catch a ride on the school ferry. Later I'd have a tired trudge back up the hill in the fading afternoon light. But now I loitered on my way to Sheila's house, studying the curled ferns, the sparkle of ice crystals on the moss. I passed through the boundary gate and onto Dodge Cove's broad path, strolling past houses topped with woodsmoke corkscrews. Sheila's path in early spring was still bereft of flowers, but slender snowdrop blades and crocus tips were emerging through the seaweed mulch.

Dolly and Christiane had hiked the muskeg trail from Crippen Cove. Opening big knapsacks, they unpacked salad greens and sewing baskets, dainty rolls of shrimp sushi, and big puffy bundles of quilting. I unloaded my salad and wine, and the fine black shoes with silver buckles a friend had offered me that sadly did not fit. "Who wants these?" I asked. Marty stepped into them, a delighted Cinderella. Then Karen said, "I've got a pair of size seven Nikes to give away," and Sheila smiled happily.

The Dodge Cove path stretched from one end of the village to the other. Goods were wheel-barrowed home from the dock, or sometimes transported by small all-terrain vehicles. Folks usually walked. Photo by Garry Sattich.

My square for Dolly's quilt was based on a photo of Dolly in her flower garden. All the squares in her quilt featured flowers, fruits or vegetables that Dolly grew.

Food was spread on counters, and quilts were spread in glory on the shining floor. Marie's quilt was nearly finished, and so was Aurianne's quilt for her teacher. Emily's baby quilt was ready to be layered. We shifted and shuffled and rearranged the squares for Carol's quilt and peeked surreptitiously into the bag of squares for Dolly's still secret quilt. We huddled stealthily in a side-room to marvel and worry over the strange needlework we had collected to make a surprise quilt for Marty's little son Kai. We were happy to just talk quilts, to admire and plan quilts, but we sensibly decided not to tackle any serious quilting. "Today is not a quilting day," someone said. "It's International Women's Day. It's a party." We filled our glasses and plates and settled down to talk about jobs, kids, gardens, storms.

"I'm so bored looking at dead fish," declared Sheila, who had the often-thankless job of validating the catches on commercial fishing boats. "I'd sure like to do something different but..."; she waved her hand in a circle. She was working to pay for the house and boat, new clothes for her boys and tuition for herself.

This photo of Dolly in her garden is what inspired me to make an appliquéd Dolly surrounded by 3-D fabric flowers as my contribution to her quilt. Photo by Garry Sattich.

The subject shifted to the college classes that she and many of the other women were taking. Francine, pale and wan after a bout of flu and her psychology class exams, spoke of her struggles to study in English, her excitement and pleasure in learning, her hopes that a diploma would open new doors, perhaps to teaching French. Wendy, who had just completed her schooling to become a teacher, smiled wryly, feeling frustrated at the lack of job offers, feeling stuck with substitute teaching. Carol, who had been a full-time teacher for years, wished for a little time off.

Out in the cold sunshine on the porch, the women were talking of gardens and housebuilding, of children and sex. One said, "Well, my nine-year-old asked me, 'What is oral sex?' He had heard about it on TV or from the other kids. I told him and he said, 'That's really gross. You don't do that, do you?'" The women rocked with laughter.

Back inside, Dolly shared how she and her partner had recently and reluctantly decided to move to town until their teenaged sons finished school. "We have to be in town for the kids to be involved in school and sports and to have normal friendships. Crippen is great for young kids, but as teenagers, their friends and activities are all in town. I wasn't happy being the taxi service taking them back and forth across the harbour," she said.

Other women nodded in agreement; they too were now scheduling their lives around their children's town activities. The irony was that so many of them had rebelled against their conventional urban upbringing by running away to the wild west coast, and now their kids were rebelling against the rural paradise where they had been raised, longing instead for the bright pleasures of town.

When Dolly left to hike back to Crippen Cove, we unpacked the blocks for the quilt we were making to celebrate her prodigious garden, her outrageously gifted green thumb. Sheila's square was an appliquéd vegetable patch, with 3-D cabbages, and carrots popping a centimetre out of the brown velvet earth. I confessed to my friends that Dolly's quilt wasn't totally a secret to her anymore. One day when she was visiting, she spotted my square for her quilt, an appliqué based on a photo of her in her garden. "That's really neat. What's it for?" she asked. I was afraid she would recognize the calico woman as herself. "Oh, it's just something I'm playing with. It's a—it's—mmm…" I said. Dolly smiled, her eyes gazing deep into mine. "Oh!" she said.

Our Women's Day party ended, and I walked along to Karen's house, then offered to take her Nikes back to Sheila. Dave asked me how big my feet were because he had a pair of steel-toed work boots to give away. I tried them on and walked out the door stiffly shod and ankle-laced. When I dropped the runners off at Sheila's, she laughed and said: "It's been a day for shoes." Climbing the hill in the chilly dusk, my strong new boots ringing on the frozen ground, I reflected on what a splendid day it had been for friendship.

⁓⁕

The women were laughing, talking, running their hands over the freshly painted woodwork, wandering through the clean empty rooms of Christiane's new home in Prince Rupert. We were gathered for a surprise house-warming party. Christiane looked so pretty, so carefree. I was used to seeing her at the dock in town, looking stoic and drawn, having just crossed the harbour in a storm, or getting ready to go back across to Crippen Cove in the dark of night.

"I'm really brave; I do what I have to do," she had told me a few months before, when I visited her at Crippen. She described her commuting routine—ironing and folding her nurse's uniform, packing it in a plastic bag; pulling in the heavy skiff. "I wear big gumboots and layers of clothing to keep me warm, and I'm wrapped in rubber from head to toe, like a big condom. I change clothes at the hospital; I'd be too wrinkled and sweaty if I wore my uniform under my rain gear."

Looking around her shiny town kitchen, I remembered sitting at her kitchen table in Crippen as water dripped from the ceiling. Christiane just moved the table, saying, "All these drips and this damn leaky roof! I wonder sometimes why I moved here." Her lilting accent softened the words, took away the sting. "Well, why did you?" I asked.

"For a small community and for country life," she said. "I was planning to have another baby, and this was a way I could afford to stay home with the kids. There's a kind of freedom here—we can have animals, there's more room; it's a great place for kids to grow up."

It was now a decade since she had moved to Crippen Cove with her partner and her young daughter Auriane. She worked full-time in town, commuting from the island by boat until she was seven months pregnant. Though she worked in a hospital, her daughter Elize was born at home. "I had my first baby at home too," she told me. "I'd attended other home births and was a nurse, so I felt capable and comfortable to give birth at home." When Elize was born, it was cold, and her partner was busy heating the house and dealing with frozen pipes. She smiled. "Usually, husbands boil water, but mine was thawing it."

I have an image in my mind, of Christiane at a quilting day when Elize was perhaps six months old. It was sunny, and we were quilting outside on the porch. Elize balanced herself easily on her mother's lap, happy in the circle of her mother's arms as Christiane concentrated on her stitches. Two-year-old Auriane sat in the sunshine with needle and thread, stringing buttons for a necklace. By age eleven and thirteen, the girls had their own sewing machine and were quilters themselves, making squares for our community quilts.

On my visit to Crippen Cove, we talked while Christiane did the dishes, ladling hot water from a big pan on the wood stove. The plumbing was a mix of rustic and modern—an electric boat pump moved rainwater from a tote outside beneath the eaves to an oak wine barrel perched over the kitchen sink. Christiane told me, "Crippen is great for little kids, but it's not a good place for teenagers. They feel trapped here, and different from the other kids. Teenagers don't like to feel different. With one teenager, and another kid who wants to be one, there's pressure on us to be closer to the action. Sometimes we think of moving to town."

I hadn't taken her seriously when she spoke of moving. But she really did it! She rented a house with high ceilings, dazzling white walls, endless stretches of clean carpeting. She really was brave, knowing what she and her daughters needed, and choosing a new life in town.

Aside from all the women gathered, her new home was almost empty—January was not a good month to be moving furniture by boat, but the place already had a comfortable, homey feel. Christiane looked serene and content; her girls smiled dreamily as they ran their fingers through the rose-coloured carpet.

We all kept touching the clean, well-tended surfaces of the house—such a contrast to most of our homes across the harbour. I think we were all a little envious. And with darkness falling and the wind rising, we could see the charm of a warm, dry house in town. "Gale warning tonight," predicted Marie. "It was already getting rough when I came over."

"I still miss living across the harbour," said Dolly, who had shocked us six months earlier when she and her family moved to town after living for eighteen years at Crippen Cove. "But I don't miss crossing the harbour on nights like this."

We began talking about our ailments, our sense that we are losing strength and vigour, that we were wearing out. "I feel like my body lets me down now," Marie said. "It doesn't want to do the things it used to, like pick up a twenty-horse motor." We laughed in agreement and someone quipped, "or even a four-horse motor." Francine told us she was having her foot x-rayed. "The doctor thinks it's arthritis." The way she said the word with a Quebecois intonation—air-trih-tihss—made her affliction sound beautiful, like an exotic flower from a faraway land.

Sheila and I got ready to leave; she had to pick up her son. Pulling on my rain pants and boots, I pictured myself staying at Christiane's, sleeping peacefully on a soft, thick carpet, walking downtown for a latte in the morning. But we said our goodbyes and headed out.

At the dock, the rigging of a hundred fishboats was making that high, fast, clattering whistle that meant the wind was very strong. Wendy, our friend from Dodge Cove, was huddled in the phone booth with her three life-jacketed daughters as the rain sluiced down. She had to yell over the wind: "We tried to get home, but we turned back. It's really rough! We're waiting for a taxi—we're going to stay in town tonight." I imagined saying, "Yeah, maybe I will too," but instead I headed down the ramp and followed Sheila to her skiff. I pulled on my floater pants, zipped up my floater coat.

Sheila's son balanced on the rail, clowning and joking as he untied the skiff. I was relieved to see that his life jacket was securely fastened. "Let's call Dad and tell him we drowned, okay? Do you think we could fool him?" he asked happily as we left the breakwater. We hurtled slowly through the darkness and the tumultuous waves in Sheila's big sturdy boat. We were halfway across, plunging and pummelled by the storm, when Sheila exclaimed, "I've never been out in weather like this."

"Never?" I asked. I knew she travelled frequently in storms and in the dark. She sometimes made three or four trips a day, going to work or to meetings, taking the kids to dancing class and hockey practice and birthday parties, attending classes herself. She usually disregarded the weather. "Really never?" I asked, thinking of an unnerving trip I once made with her outside the harbour in a little speedboat, while breakers crashed ruthlessly on the rocks all around us.

"Well, never in this boat," she said as a great wave broke over the bow. I pictured the rosy carpet again, the cup of steaming latte. "I'm glad you're with me tonight," Sheila declared. "The waves and the wind are really weird." I felt like reminding her of what she had said as we were driving to the dock: "There's no weather this boat can't take." But I didn't say anything. I hoped that she was right. "I'm glad you're the captain," I told her.

Living By the Tides

The rise and fall of the tides were on my mind as I entered the half-filled bowl of Crippen Cove at mid-tide on a windy, blustery day. Three hours to low tide. I didn't want to go dry. Where should I tie my boat? Dolly's clothesline was long and hard to pull; Marie's was shorter, but her float was slanting sideways, pushed by the wind. I eased my skiff up to the newest "dock," made of logs lashed side by side and tethered to the shore, hoping there would be water underneath when I wanted to leave. I clambered onto the slippery, tippy logs, grateful for the gritty traction of nailed-on roofing scraps, then crossed the gravel beach and climbed the steps to Wendy and Kevin's house.

The original tiny, low-ceilinged cabin was now Wendy's kitchen, with a larger, newer house built around it. The room, with its antiquated brown wainscotting, was warm and fragrant. Wood stove and electric range stood

At high tide, Crippen Cove was lovely. Water filled the cove, and Wendy could tie her boat to a log dock right in front of her house.

back-to-back. Clumps of drying herbs hung from nails in the ceiling beams, and a batch of newly moulded soap was hardening on the counter. A steep, ladder-like stairway angled sharply upward along one wall.

Wendy gazed out her kitchen window at an idyllic salt water scene, waves lapping at a rocky shore, houses perched on pilings, a profusion of flowers, the dark forest behind. She was keeping track of things: the kids, the tide, the boats, the seaweed, the weather, the comings and goings of her neighbours. Her focus was the tide, the twice-daily rising and falling of the tide, the ancient moon-driven mechanism that activated and regulated life at Crippen Cove.

At low tide, the water was sucked right out of the cove, leaving a broad expanse of deep black mud, a few boulders, and deadheads. Skiffs lay stranded in the sea-reeking muck. Little kids in gumboots splashed with oozy pleasure in a shallow skim of water. The houses were six metres above the muddy flats, perched like toys on the rim of an empty pie pan smeared with chocolate pudding. At low tide, the cove looked tawdry and dishevelled.

But at high tide, Crippen Cove was anyone's idea of paradise. Sparkling water, a narrow edge of beach, waves rippling to the bottom step of a front porch with a wooden rowboat tied to the railing. At high tide, angel-faced children in tightly cinched orange life jackets with big angel-wing

On a low tide, Crippen Cove is a vast expanse of mud, rocks and seaweed, and the only way to get to shore is to wade through the gumboot-sucking mud.

collars balanced on the floating logs or pretended to row the tied-up boats. In the summer, orange-bellied kids waded or swam in the cold, cold water until their teeth clattered.

Wendy explained: "They have to wear floaters or life jackets if they're on the beach at high tide. If they're fishing off the dock or playing in the boats, they have to wear floaters. They have boundaries where they are allowed, and wherever they are, I can see them." She offered me a plate of cookies and pointed to a rocky outcropping. "They can take their raft over to the rocks, but that's as far as they can go. If they want to go farther, they have to put their life jackets on. They learn the rules of the beach and the docks pretty young here."

She told me how Bobby, at age five, put on his life jacket and rowed out after a ball floating away on the tide. "He rowed out there and got the ball; he can row, but not really well. The wind was blowing and he couldn't row back in, so he threw over the anchor to keep from drifting out of the cove, and one of the kids came and got me to help him."

The children at Crippen Cove seemed to live in great freedom, roaming the beaches in a pack, swinging from a tire in the woods, snitching strawberries from every garden. A child could walk into any of the households in the cove, and ask for dry socks or a slice of bread and butter. The kids knew that any grown-up would give them a Band-Aid, a glass of juice, or a comforting hug. The mothers phoned from house to house all day, keeping track of the kids, who seemed oblivious to this close surveillance.

Wendy laughed. "One day my neighbour phoned me. 'Are you missing a kid,' she asked. He'd only been out of my sight for ten minutes, but he'd opened her door and was looking at the fish tank when she came home from work. Dolly found him at her place once. He'd gone to get cookies and knew exactly where the cookie jar was."

The women at Crippen Cove formed a tight, warm sisterhood, sharing an intense interest in gardening and the natural world, amiably and nonchalantly tending each other's children, and migrating from house to house for the daily coffee break. Wendy and her friend Sandy made baskets together, casually sharing the task. One might lay the framework of spokes, and the other interweave the strands of dried grass and reed, or add bits of seaweed or multicoloured moss.

As in any small community, neighbours sometimes squabbled or disagreed, but they still kept an informal eye out for each other in stormy weather, and worked together to improve trails and to repair the docks and clotheslines. "If you need a ride, you just phone around to see who's going to town," Wendy said. "Or you ask them to buy some milk for you, or to pick up your kid, or whatever you need. But it's still pretty private here too. We all have our own interests; everybody lives their own lives."

She took me upstairs to see the quilt of butterflies and flowers that she had just finished for her daughter. Hidden inside the new covering was a well-loved but worn-out baby quilt that her friends had made for her a decade before. It was now the secret heart of Amber's new quilt, as the friendships of the women themselves were the secret heart of Crippen Cove.

Wendy once came to a Halloween party dressed in a cardboard box, her face beaming above the tidy knot that held the cover closed, her legs dancing out of the bottom. Right away, we all knew what she was—a tie-down. A tie-down was what you asked the clerk for when you wanted your groceries in a box with a lid, knotted tightly with shiny yellow plastic twine. It was a useful form of packaging when you had to carry groceries home by boat. The women at Crippen Cove tried to do their shopping by the tide, leaving home on a rising tide as soon as the skiff was floating, and coming back when the water was at its highest, so they could heave their tie-downs out of the boats and onto the upper shoreline, rather than having to carry the hefty boxes through the mud and slippery seaweed.

Every board and plank, every nail, all the heavy double-paned doors and windows needed for the addition Wendy and Kevin were building; it all had to be muscled ashore. She grimaced and exclaimed: "Out of the boat! Up the dock! Up the back hill, all the way to the very back of the property! I told him, 'I can't do this anymore. The next time you bring things home, you better bring someone else to help you.'" She sighed, "I used to do it and not feel totally exhausted. It's definitely age. But I'm smarter now. I've learned to manage so I don't burn myself out. I try to make it so I actually enjoy what I'm doing."

Wendy set down her teacup, checked the tide table and her watch, glanced out the kitchen window at her boat. She and her neighbours continually but almost unconsciously made complex calculations about the tides, precise to the inch and the minute. "I have to move my skiff now. I have to pick up the kids at three-thirty," she said. The school ferry dropped the children off at the airport dock a kilometre away, and the parents took turns picking them up.

To make sure that her boat would still be floating when it was time to leave, Wendy needed to move it into deeper water. She slipped on her gumboots and headed for the log dock. Moving the skiff to the very end of the dock gave her the half hour and the depth of water she needed. She repositioned her boat, then threw out a heavy lead "cannonball" anchor to keep it from drifting back in.

As I watched her out the window, I remembered talking to Shelley's partner Bill about miscalculating the falling tide. "Oh, it's torture!" he had said. "There is nothing more frustrating than pushing a boat down the beach a fraction of a second slower than the tide is dropping. You take the motor off and put it somewhere out of the mud, then push the boat out, then carry the motor through the muck back to the boat!"

But Wendy had moved her boat to deep water in time, outwitting the tide. Back in the house, she tried to explain her ongoing decision-making process. She pointed to a pink mooring buoy far outside the cove and said, "For example, if I have to leave for work at five a.m., and at 5:05 the tide will be three-point-nine feet, then my skiff has to be tied to that buoy out there. Otherwise, I can't go. The dock goes dry at twelve feet, the clothesline goes dry at four feet, so they're no good on a three-point-nine." If she guessed wrong about where to tie her boat, she'd be stranded by the tide and late for work.

"Your boat's still good for ten minutes," she commented, noticing my frequent glances at the falling water. What she meant was that my boat would be stuck in the mud if I didn't leave right away. It was time to go. As I said goodbye, Wendy asked me to tug on the anchor rope as I passed her boat, to pull it a little deeper, giving her an extra few centimetres, an extra minute or two before she had to leave.

Heading out of the cove, I imagined the moon goddess at her celestial sewing machine, endlessly sewing zigzag stitches. The peak of the zig was the high tide, the valley of the zag the low tide, with two complete

Our community food order is arriving at Dodge Cove by boat. Boxes, buckets, and fifty-pound sacks of bulk food are piled on the deck of Bill T.'s fishboat, the *Hi-Lo*.

zigzag stitches each day creating the twice-daily rise and fall of the water. Throughout her monthly cycle, the moon goddess gradually turned the stitch-width dial as she sewed. At the full moon, the knob was turned to its greatest width to produce the big tides that lapped at the cedar branches overhanging the shore, and then fell more than six metres to reveal the scurrying crabs of the depths. As the moon waned, the moon goddess slowly diminished the width of her zigzag stitch, creating the undramatic two- to three-metre tides of mid-cycle.

When I reached the choppy waves of the deeper outer channel, I abandoned my daydream and revved up the outboard. Wendy in her silver speedboat zipped past me with a regal wave and a broad moon goddess smile, right on time to pick up the kids.

On Distribution Day, the food came to us at high tide. Boxes, buckets, and twenty-five-kilogram bags were piled on the deck of the gallant little *Hi-Lo*. The cargo included cheese, dried fruit, beans, and rice, but most precious were the chocolate chips and the four-kilogram sacks of the dark French coffee that fuelled the cove. The "hoofers" had met the freight truck from Vancouver at the dock in town and had packed the food down the ramp to the bright orange fishboat. A bottle of olive oil was accidently dropped overboard as they hurried to catch the tide.

At Dodge Cove, we waited in Dave and Karen's boat shed for the food to arrive. The shed was as big as a high school gym, but had only three walls. The centre of the roof was open to the sky, replicating the cut-out space in the floor below. Boats came into the shed through the open front when the tide was high, and nestled between two dock-like platforms, with their masts projecting through the empty space in the roof.

As the food-laden boat eased its way inside, Karen reached down for the tie-up lines and looped them around stout pilings. Any other boat would be level with the boat shed floor, but the *Hi-Lo* was so small that those aboard had to heft the boxes and bags up to us, as we stretched down to grab them. We were the "splitters," who would divide the bulk food into smaller portions for each family.

We piled up the food in the midst of vast nautical clutter. There was stuff everywhere, formidable bandsaws and acetylene torches, giant winches and planers. Shards of aluminum littered the floor where Dave was welding a new afterdeck for his troller, which loomed in the back of the boat shed. Anchors, driveshafts and cleats mingled with a scant overlay of discarded household objects on a nine-metre long workbench.

The makeshift tables Karen had set up were more elegant than usual. A freshly varnished hatch cover balanced on sawhorses, and a huge gleaming

At Dave and Karen's boat shed in Dodge Cove, arms reach down to receive the boxes of food being lifted from the boat.

slab of aluminum was supported by packing crates. There was even an old table that had floated in on the tide.

I helped Francine and Karen unpack the boxes and divide the food that was easy to split into what each household had purchased, while Wendy checked and re-checked the order forms. The splitters would take some of the bulk containers home—things like the twelve-kilogram boxes of raisins and the twenty-litre bucket of dish soap were easier to split and repackage in a tidy kitchen. But a mix of laziness and nostalgia made me want to do my splitting in the boat shed, as we had so often done before.

I lingered at the shiny aluminum table, pouring vanilla extract into small bottles, filling ice-cream buckets with split peas. I scrupulously divided the dried cherries without eating more than three or four and poured streams of yellow parmesan into quart canning jars. I was reminded of how Thanksgiving is supposed to feel—bountiful, abundant.

Distribution Day had been part of my life for years. We used to call it D-day, back when we called ourselves the Slack Tide Co-op and ordered our food from Fed Up Cooperative Wholesale in Vancouver. I first met many of the quilters, though they weren't quilters yet, at Slack Tide meetings when I still lived in town. One of the women almost had her baby at a Slack Tide meeting at Fisherman's Hall, when her water broke as she climbed the steps.

Makeshift tables have been set up in the boat shed, where Karen and others will divide the food, working from a list of what each family has ordered.

Later, we held our meetings and D-days in an old Cow Bay rope loft with baffling metal objects still bolted to the floor and air still reeking of tar. On a rare sunny day, after I had moved to Salt Lakes, we held the meeting outside and Lorrie took off all her clothes to sunbathe as we wrote up the food order.

The days of Slack Tide and Fed Up were long gone; by 1995, we were only a "buying club" ordering from a sadly diminished catalogue. But the sense of bounty, of overflowing plenitude, came back as I divided a 4.5-kilogram block of extra old cheddar and Karen poured chocolate chips into paper bags. We only ate a few.

Older Now

We were young for so very long, when we lived in the rain-washed cabins at Salt Lakes and Crippen Cove. For many years my community of friends seemed effortlessly, endlessly young, somehow outside the constraints of time. We couldn't believe we were growing older. But by 1995, strands of grey had invaded the heads bent over the quilting table; we squinted to thread a needle.

On quilting days, we still shared the intimacies and complexities of our lives, but oddly, there was one topic we seemed to avoid. Menopause. Nobody wanted to talk about it. Someone might tentatively mention the subject, but there would be a subdued lack of response instead of our usual lively discussion.

One day a friend called me, "I need to talk to you about menopause. We never talk about it." After a startled silence, I agreed: "You're right. I don't even like to think about it. I just want to ignore it as long as I can."

"I can't ignore it," she said. "I think I'm going crazy."

I said soothingly, "Oh, you're not going crazy."

"Thanks!" she said, in a tight, tearful voice, and hung up the phone. Her words and her pain stayed with me as I thought about menopause and my reactions to it for the next few days. If I wasn't so busy ignoring it, I'd acknowledge that my periods were waning and that I was often very warm. I'd admit that my moods see-sawed and ricocheted; that I sometimes felt ferocious depletions of energy, a slow shrivelling of vitality.

I should have asked my friend what she was feeling, in body and in spirit. I should have told her that I was sometimes taut with anxiety, feeling like an over-blown balloon at the end of a fraying string, or else deflated, without resilience or joyful bounce. I should have told her that I often felt crazy too—jittery and splintered, volatile and easily enraged. Taking the metaphor of the balloon any further meant picturing myself as an empty, wrinkled, pastel blob lying useless and forgotten in a dusty corner. No wonder I couldn't help or comfort someone else.

Many of the women I knew had reached middle age—not really old yet, but starting to joke about bifocals, sore backs, lapses of memory. Women who were wild and rebellious in their youth, who ran away from home themselves, now worried about their teenagers borrowing the skiff without asking and wondered how to keep their kids from going wild.

I didn't envy my friends anymore, the way I had when their children were small. I was glad I wasn't the parent of a teenager. By this time, my friends were a bit jealous of me, for the freedom of summer-long boat trips and for the quiet simplicity of my life. I wasn't tied down to mortgage payments or the need to buy eighty-dollar running shoes for two or three sets of growing feet. Sheila told me: "You've held on to the lifestyle we're all pining for. With kids, our decisions have so much more depending on them. We can't live day-to-day anymore without a paycheque."

The women were on the fast track, whether they liked it or not. They zipped across the harbour at all hours, in all weather, in expensive speed-boats that they needed to earn money to pay for. They worked in town to cover the mortgages on the houses they and their partners were building or remodelling. They had computers now and went back to school to better themselves in order to get higher paying jobs. They flew home for hasty or lengthy visits with ailing parents and the siblings who had responsibly stayed close enough to help their folks in their old age.

Having moved far from our childhood homes and the burden of our parents' expectations, we now paid the price of feeling guilty as our parents aged and died with too little help from us. We worried about them, agonized long distance, visited when we could. On quilting days, we shared the milestones of our parents' declining health. "We used to talk about sex and drugs," one of the quilters commented. "Then later on, we talked about babies and how to raise our kids. Now we talk about our fathers' strokes and heart attacks or our mothers' dementia."

When I lived at Salt Lakes, I'd visit my family once or twice a year. Now I was making the long trip from Dodge Cove to Seattle every few months because my mother needed me. She was bent double with osteoporosis and pinned to a wheelchair with a broken hip, her mind clouded and confused. Each visit, I stunned myself into exhaustion trying to be the dutiful daughter, doting on her for a week or two, trying to make up for my absence, to make up for lost time. I did everything I could, except what she needed and wanted most. I didn't move back to Seattle. I didn't give up my life in the north.

On my way home from Seattle, I often stopped overnight at Lorrie's in Vancouver. The quilting circle there had made a quilt for a friend with AIDS. "It's not an AIDS quilt," Lorrie said, meaning that it was not a commemorative panel for the huge Names Project. It was a real quilt, soft, warm, and comforting. Another Vancouver quilt for a sick friend had a square with an appliquéd coil of silver-grey satin intestines. The quilter was wishing the recipient shiny new guts that would work better than his damaged innards.

I told Lorrie about the quilt we had made to honour a friend who had drowned and tried to paraphrase what his widow had written to us:

"I love this quilt. It often comforted me when I was grieving. It is a solid and heartfelt symbol of the web of love and friendship that supported me in that time of sorrow, and it connects me still to the community of friends and family."

North and south, our lives and our concerns had become more serious, and the focus of our quilt-making had altered and broadened. We still made baby quilts and birthday quilts, but we made quilts for more sombre reasons too. We didn't take life for granted anymore. We were older now, and it seemed there was more at stake.

I was still rocking with the clickety-click of the train ride as I stepped out of the taxi into a shimmer of afternoon sunshine. I'd been gone all summer sailing with Iain through the green wilderness solitude of the BC coast. Then I spent a week in Seattle with my ailing mother and a few lovely days at Lorrie's in Vancouver before a two-day train ride through the dusty heart of the province.

I hitchhiked a ride to Dodge Cove with Jane, who was clambering over a fishboat with briefcase in hand, to reach *Lollipop*, her little speedboat. Looking colourfully dignified in her work clothes of tailored red blazer and flowered skirt, she zipped up her bulky life jacket vest and started the motor. "You're a wonderful sight, so elegant and seaworthy," I said. I teased her about her boat shoes; polished black low-heeled pumps that contrasted oddly with the weathered deck of her boat. "Hey, they have rubber soles. Non-skid!" she said, then invited me for tea on Sunday.

All week I greeted friends and shared the tales of summer. A mother shouted hello in the clear dusk at Marine Bay, where the Dodge Cove path dead-ended onto the beach. She and her three daughters were camping, fifteen minutes from their house. They had spent much of the summer there, often joined by other cove moms and kids. "It's a great way to camp," she said. "If you've forgotten something, or if it starts raining, you just go home."

When I stopped by to see Carol, she was swinging an axe, splitting huge rounds of firewood. Dozens of massive rounds loomed behind her, higher than her head. "Looks like you have your work cut out for you," I joked.

Margo and her family were house-sitting for a month down in the cove. Every summer they came back north to reunite with old friends, to can their winter supply of salmon, and to celebrate Dylan's birthday on the beach. The splashing, swimming kids at the birthday party didn't seem to mind the frigid water. A child proudly showed me her hand: "Look," she said, "I can't move my little finger! It's too cold!"

Carol is chopping firewood from the beachcombed logs Bill S. has hauled up from the shore. They have cut and stacked the great rounds of wood, which will be split and stacked in the woodshed to the right. Photo by Garry Sattich.

Margo and her sons, now aged ten and twelve, hiked up to visit. It had been six years since they lived on CBC Hill and played in the little shed that their dad and grandpa had built at the edge of the lawn. The red and white open-sided play-shed was still stocked with their toys: the aluminum helicopter that Hans had welded, the bathtub toys that migrated outdoors, the little plastic beach shovel now dwarfed by Dylan's sun-browned hand. Galen had to stoop to avoid hitting his head. "I remember this! Here's my dolphin! Here's my boat!" The boys noticed that fine golden sand had replaced the old gravelly sand. They hunkered down briefly, happy to scoop up sand with the plastic bulldozers of their childhood, but then wandered inside to play computer games.

Summer was almost over and I had to go back to work. I ironed a shirt, pinned up my hair and hiked down to our dock. I was happy to be in my yellow skiff again, bounding slowly over the kindly waves. I sank again into the familiar routines and duties of my job, and reconnected with the people there. When I got in line at the credit union, I was surrounded by an odorous payday crowd of gumbooted and overalled cannery workers. Marie and Francine, near the head of the line, flashed me wide smiles. "You're back! How was your summer?"

I imagined that the dozen people who stood between us were listening with interest as we exchanged our summer stories. Marie reached the teller and conducted her business, then came back to give me a kiss and a hug. The line inched forward. Francine finished her banking and joined me, giving me a kiss Quebecois-style, right on the mouth.

"I keep getting kissed in the bank today," I exclaimed, a bit embarrassed because of the long line of dour people glimpsed over her shoulder. Francine beamed. "What better place to be kissed?" she asked, her brown eyes shining.

Drifting towards sleep one night, I was startled awake by the radio newscast. A woman in Montreal had given birth to a baby after an abdominal pregnancy. I'd never heard the words "abdominal pregnancy" said aloud except long ago by my own amazed doctors. Or on the rare occasions when I said them myself: "I had an abdominal pregnancy. Like an ectopic pregnancy, only much worse."

Speaking hesitantly, almost ashamedly, trying to explain something I didn't understand myself: "The baby wasn't in the uterus; it was growing right in my belly and I was bleeding to death without knowing it. The doctors didn't know until I collapsed. I had an emergency operation and that was the end of the baby."

But this Montreal woman's baby was born alive, just last week. She and her doctor hadn't known either, until her Caesarian delivery. Apparently her baby is healthy, unaffected by its novel beginnings. I had been told that mine couldn't have grown to term; that even if it had somehow miraculously been born, it would have been severely damaged.

It—that's how I think of it now—a neutral little blob that didn't see life. Misbegotten. At the time, it wasn't an It. It was my tragically lost baby that I couldn't even say was lost, the baby I couldn't say had died, because it had never even lived. Secretly, I had held myself responsible. I had felt like a freak, felt myself to be secretly, inwardly inhospitable to new life.

Recently I've seen books focusing on the emotional pain of losing an unborn child, on the devastation of a lost pregnancy, but the Rupert library didn't have books like that when I needed them. There are support groups in Rupert now dealing with grief and loss that would have helped me back then. But I've dealt with things in my own way, I've been sustained by friends, and comforted by the healing passage of time.

It was odd, though, like the breaking of a taboo, to hear the announcer say the words "abdominal pregnancy" on the radio. I wanted to tell him that "that's what happened to me." I had felt so solitary, so horrifically unique, as though I were suffering from an unknown disease, or was the last survivor of a previously undiscovered tribe.

I had looked up my condition in medical books, had read the statistics and a few case histories, but that wasn't like hearing about the woman in Montreal, a real person whose experience was somewhat similar to mine, though with a happier ending. I wonder how she views her pregnancy. As a miracle? Or a medical oddity? Does she feel lucky, or afflicted, or just stupendously surprised?

Our short stint house-sitting for Margo and Hans had stretched into ten years as caretakers on CBC Hill, but by 1998, the transmitter equipment had been automated, and there was little need for caretakers on-site. We began to think about leaving, though there seemed no need to hurry. It took more than a year before we decided to move to Gabriola Island on the Salish Sea, across Georgia Strait from Vancouver, and nearer to our families.

Moving from CBC Hill was arduous. Everything we owned came precariously down the hill on the tiny ATV, load after endless load, then was carried down the ramp to be packed into a Budget rental van we had brought from town by barge. When the van was full, we stuffed the rest into our new sailboat. We would take the van south, then come back for a last voyage down the wilderness coast. I would be leaving my dear friends, the community quilting, the quiet and peaceful surrounding—and my skiff,

Moving from CBC Hill was very hard work. Every object had to be carried down the dock ramp and loaded aboard a rental truck we had brought from town by barge. Our new sailboat is tied on the other side of the dock.

This is the last quilting day I attended before moving south. Dolly and Sheila D. are stitching. I was very aware of how much I would miss them and all the friends I was leaving behind. Photo by Lonnie Wishart.

Before I left, I wanted to update the charts and files documenting our twenty years of quilting together. Sheila S., Dolly, Jane, myself, Wendy Bo, Christiane, and Karen are going through this material. Photo by Lonnie Wishart.

which had to be sold. I felt guiltily ambivalent about moving south only after my parents had passed away, but it was the inheritance they had left me, added to Iain's book royalties, that enabled us to buy a home on Gabriola Island.

On my last quilting day at the schoolhouse, I wore the sterling silver brooch my island friends had given me as a farewell gift. It had been made by Des, who described the intricate, garnet-studded Celtic design as a powerful talisman of strength and courage. The day was filled with hugs, wine, stitching, and remembrance. Quilts were photographed and the chart listing quilts and quilters was updated. It was a colourful, happy, sad day, and I was intensely aware of how much I would miss these women, the sisters of my heart.

It's Not the End of the Story

When Iain and I left Dodge Cove in 2000, I packed away an unfinished manuscript, the many chapters I had envisioned becoming a book. I boxed up the interviews I had done with my friends, along with photos of quilts and quilting days, of boats, babies, cabins, and coves. Taping up the cartons, I sealed away the documentation and remembrances of two decades of my life in the north. By that time, more than fifty community quilts had been made, with over a hundred people involved. But I stopped keeping track when we moved to Gabriola Island in southern BC. The quilting circle continued to make beautiful and meaningful gifts for friends, but I gave up trying to document its communal creativity.

Life was easier on Gabriola. No muddy paths, no stormy commutes by boat. Our boating was now recreational, no longer essential, and we seldom ventured far. Our former summer voyages, our grand and perilous adventures on the sea, were abandoned in favour of short trips in sheltered waters. Self-described as the "Isle of the Arts," Gabriola nurtured our creativity. Iain flourished as a writer of best-selling books for children and youth. I explored the far reaches of art quilting, sold and exhibited my quilts,

The quilting continued, of course, after I left. Sheila S., Jane, Karen, and Wendy Bo are stitching on Lou's quilt at the Dodge Cove schoolhouse in 2007.

and taught workshops. I founded an activist quilt group that tackled environmental issues with group-made protest quilts.

And of course, I continued making quilts with my friends, the Coastal Quilters, sending my contributions back to the northern women or over to the Vancouver group. In 2008, friends from north, south, and east gathered on Gabriola for a weekend quilting bee, taking me back to our old rambunctious quilting days. I was

Madoka, myself, and Elisha are working on Luca's quilt in 2008, when some of my dear quilting friends and their daughters gathered at my home on Gabriola Island.

touched that a younger generation of quilters joined us. Shelley's daughters, Mia and Chloe, and Lorrie's daughter Elisha and her friend worked on a baby quilt for Francine's grandson.

Iain and I separated in 2017, and I moved from Gabriola to Powell River, a small city on the Salish Sea. I hid my troublesome boxes of writing and photos under the bed and tried to ignore them. But a year ago, Jane finally convinced me to haul them out of their dusty hiding place, though I didn't want to do it. Those boxes represented failure to me, the abandonment of a project that was once dear to my heart.

Jane is a retired nurse and hospital administrator. She is energetic, sociable, well-organized, and she gets things done. When she lived in Dodge Cove, she hosted tea parties where she cut our hair, advised us on medical issues, fed us homemade almond roca and tried unsuccessfully to teach us how to get organized with daily/weekly/yearly planners. With the vet's blessing, she tenderly euthanized the ancient dogs of the cove so they didn't have to endure a boat ride to town.

Feeling that it was important to record women's stories, in 2014, Jane invited northern friends and acquaintances to write about their lives. She compiled the memoirs of thirty-four women, including myself and twenty of the quilters, into *Gumboot Girls: Adventure, Love, and Survival on British Columbia's North Coast*, a book that became a surprise bestseller. When she moved south, she compiled a second book, *Dancing in Gumboots: Adventure, Love and Resilience: Women of the Comox Valley*. Lou, who is part of our quilting circle and the northern saltwater community, edited both books.

The launch party for *Gumboot Girls* in 2015 was a joyous event. Twenty of the women in our quilting circle had contributed chapters that told of their experiences living on the north coast in the seventies.

Now Jane wanted to create an online database and an archive to document our forty years of group-made quilts. She had her own boxes of photos and files—after I moved south, she and Carol had taken over the task of keeping track of the quilts, documenting who they were made for and why, and who worked on them. "We're getting older," she said. "We need to deal with all this stuff before we die, or it will probably get thrown out in the trash." Jane wanted photos and facts, especially about the early quilts, and she knew that many of the images and answers were hidden in my boxes, and in the hours of video that Anneke had recorded with Lorrie's help.

At her urging, I finally excavated my boxes and unpacked the past. Dreading to look at my abandoned manuscript, I picked up a chapter at random, and was drawn back into what suddenly seemed the most vital, magical, and venturesome years of my life. Reading what I had written so long ago, I knew that I needed and wanted to finish the book, the book you are now reading.

But I was perplexed, wondering how to leap over the two decades since leaving the north coast, how to shift from past to present. I was baffled by how to wrap up this complicated tale about the quilts, the quilters, and myself. According to Jane's database, our communal quilts now numbered one hundred and thirty, with several more under construction. A hundred and fifty folks had by now been swallowed by the Quilting Amoebae. Some of the people who had been given quilts when they were infants were now having babies themselves, and they and their friends and siblings were joining the group quilt-making process to welcome this new generation.

Several new ways of making quilts together have been introduced over the years. In 2004, Jane initiated a process she dubbed "The Kristinite Challenge" in my honour. The idea was for a group of women to commit to working on each other's quilts, in a tightly scheduled and structured version of our old leisurely pass-the-medallion approach. Each woman mailed a centre square to the next person on a list. She received

Mia had been given a group-made quilt when she was a baby. Her face shows her surprise and pleasure as she unfolds a communally made quilt for her infant son, Levi.

someone else's centre square and had a month to add a border to it before passing it on. Each month, the growing quilt tops were sent onward to someone else. Eventually, each woman received her centre square back, now surrounded by the contributions of all the women, and transformed into a full-size quilt top. Despite, or perhaps because of, the strict guidelines, the resulting quilts were exceptionally sophisticated, quirky, and complex. Five Challenges took place over fifteen years, resulting in forty-four stunning quilts.

Carol initiated the Dodge Cove Counting Quilts, another way for friends to make baby quilts together. Each square was based on a page from *Cove Kids Count*, written and illustrated by Pat Gordon, who had lived in Dodge Cove in the 1970s. "One boat, two herons, three crabs… eight clams, nine seagulls, ten kids." Each square was appliquéd and embroidered by a different woman, with the child's family's fishboat always depicted. Seven counting quilts have now been made, with another underway.

In 2017, Lorrie and I hosted a glorious quilting weekend in Powell River, with friends from north and south gathering to eat, drink, camp out in our yard, and work on several quilts.

Karen's 2019 Challenge quilt is a complex and sophisticated design that developed without planning as each woman added whatever she pleased, in a series of concentric borders.

Pictorial quilts are a recent development, where folks are invited to add images to a fabric background to create a scene. A pictorial quilt for Oceane, Francine's grandchild, inspired Lorrie and me to envision a green and mossy forest quilt for Moss, Elisha's new baby. We asked friends to mail us animals and plants that we stitched to a verdant background. Embroidered birds and flowers, crocheted rabbits and a painted goat, two bears, a mushroom and a skunk cabbage, a raven, and the family dog all tumbled through the mail slot. Lorrie and I spent many afternoons arranging and rearranging these offerings, and stitching down a playful and idyllic forest scene.

Carol's quilt from the 2017 Challenge shows how far our group-made quilts have progressed since our early pass-the-medallion quilts.

I'm an old lady now, over seventy, and counting my blessings. It's been more than twenty years since I left the north coast. I live in Powell River, a small coastal city north of Vancouver, and I share a house, fruit trees, and gardens with Lorrie, my dear friend of forty-plus years. Her daughter Elisha lives next door with her husband and kids, and they have lovingly included me in their family circle.

Three years ago, I ventured into the unnerving world of online dating. "You're so brave!" exclaimed my friends. "Aren't you scared?" Yes, of course I was, but luckily, I connected with a fine, tender-hearted old fellow named John. We met a week before the first Covid restrictions were imposed and remained a strict two metres apart for the first three months of our romance, barely daring to hold hands. Then we threw caution to the winds, closed the gap, and nestled close. We have fun together, sharing a great fondness

Elisha with Moss and Malcolm. The pictorial baby quilt for Moss is on the left. Malcolm was given the two baby quilts hanging on the right.

for boats, dogs, camping, gardening, and each other.

I am a lucky woman. I pick tomatoes and talk to my cucumbers, imagining that my thumbs are turning green. Rowing my tiny skiff, a graceful dory that my sweetheart John restored for me, I enjoy the pull of the oars with John smiling in the stern and his dog lolling in the bow. My fridge is full and my bookshelves sag with stacks of books, and the city bus goes right past my front door. I hold baby Moss and gaze into her unfathomable eyes and feel blessed that she and her brother Malcolm are part of my world.

I begin to visualize the quilt square I'll make for our next community quilt, a gift to sustain a friend with cancer. Drinking tea with Lorrie and Jane, we imagine the growth of the Coastal Quilters as a flourishing and ever-branching tree. A seed was sown in 1979 when five friends who had never quilted before made a baby quilt. Forty-three years later, nourished by the love and stitches of a vast and far-flung community, our tree of quilts is lush and sturdy, and still growing strong. How fortunate I am to have been part of its growth.

John and I are dancing at the Port Townsend Wooden Boat Festival in 2022. Photo: Viviann Kuehl

Acknowledgements

I am infinitely grateful to the friends who have enriched my life, shared their stories, and trusted me to write about them. Making quilts with you has been a delight.

I am grateful to have lived in the unceded territories of the Coast Salish peoples and in the unceded territory of the Tsimshian Nation and to presently live in the traditional territory of the Tla'amin Nation.

Thank you, Jane Wilde, for encouraging me to open those boxes hidden under my bed, and for compiling an archive and slide show of the 130 quilts made by the Coastal Quilters. I am grateful for your friendship, your perseverance, and your enthusiasm.

Thank you, Lou Allison, for your friendship, and for gifting me with your editorial skills and guiding me through first and second drafts of the manuscript.

Grateful thanks to the photographers: Garry Sattich, Lonnie Wishart, Carmel Pepin, Iain Lawrence, Julie Moore, Marie Meynen, Claire Tangvald, and to the many others who contributed photos. The photos make the stories come alive.

I am thankful for Iain Lawrence's drawing, for the painting by Cheryl Hutcheson, for the poems of Carol Manning and Marty Sutmoller, and for Ned Jacob's song.

I am grateful to Vici Johnstone and Sarah Corsie at Caitlin Press for turning my words into a real book, and I thank Malaika Aleba for her marketing skills. It has been a pleasure to work with all of you.

Special thanks to Jane Wilde, Lorrie Thompson, Marie Meynen, John Hannah, and Lou Allison for your unwavering support, encouragement, laughter, and your belief in the value of my writing.

Thank you to Mary Bywater Cross for recognizing the uniqueness of our quilts and suggesting I write a research paper for the American Quilt Study Group about the quilts and the community that created them.

I want to express my great appreciation and admiration for the creativity, generosity, and loving kindness of the over one hundred and fifty people who have joined the quilting circle over the decades. I wish I could have written about all of you. Your names are listed on the next page.

Quilt Gallery

Moss's Quilt, 2022

Sarah's Challenge Quilt, 2019

Galen's Quilt, 1983

Emma's Quilt, 1991 Photo: Carmel Pepin

Marie's Quilt, 1995

Emily's Quilt, 1995

Claire's Quilt, 1987   Photo: Carmel Pepin

Richard's Quilt, 2018

Rylan's Quilt, 1997

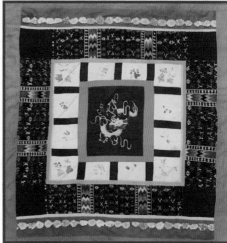

The Coastal Quilters, 1979 to 2022

The number of quilts is indicated for those who worked on five or more quilts.

Agate Annie	VerSteeg	
Allison		
Amber	Sheasgreen	
Amy	Wright	
Angenita	Gerbracht	
Anneke	Van Vliet	18
Annie	Sarazin	11
Atty	Gell	6
Auriane	Chouinard-Duggleby	9
Ava	Wagner	
Becky	Leakey	
Bergan	Jacobs	
Beth	Baron	
Beth		
Betsy	Cardell	
Bill	Smith	

Opposite:
Top left: Hayden's Quilt, 1990
Top right: Dory's Quilt, 1997
Middle left: Lorrie and Paul's Quilt, 1984
Middle right: Kai's Quilt, 1995
Bottom left: Bobby's Quilt, 1988
Bottom right: Dolly's Challenge Quilt, 2010

Boom Booms

Brandin	Lilgert	
Bronwyn	Brooks	
Carmel	Pepin	9
Carol	Brown	11
Carol	Manning	49
Carol	Bier	
Cecile	Brunelle	8
Charlotte	Darisy	
Chloe	Beam	
Chloe	Edbrooke	
Christiane	Chouinard	20
Claire	Prosser	
Claire		
Clara	Scott	
Colleen	Armstrong	
Daisy Alicia	Randall	
Danielle		
Daphne	Brown	14
David	Hinzie	
Des	Nobels	
Diane	Ricco	
Dolly	Harasym	35
Dory	Spencer	
Elisha	Manson	
Elize	Duggleby-Chouinard	8
Emily	Ramer	
Erin	Seidemann	
Eunice	Seideman	
Evanne (Uncle)		
Florence	Crozier	
Fran	Seideman	
France	Harvey	18

Francine	Masse	31
Gail	Rice	
Gene	Logan	
Ghislaine	De St Venant	22
Ginger	Talbot	17
Greg	Miller	
Heather	Truscott	
Helen	Heffernan	8
Helen	Dobie	
Iain	Lawrence	
Jan	Gardner	
Jane	Wilde	38
Janet	Gibbs	
Janet (+Bill)	Simpson	
Janice	Stonell	
Jean	LaPage	
Jeannine	Randall	
Jennifer	Kennedy	
Jennifer		
Jenny	Webster	
Jenny	Glickman	
Joanne	Webster	
John	Cross	
Jolanda	Nobels	
Joline	Martin	
Karen	Lapoint	6
Karen	McKinster	39
Karen	Talbot	
Karen	Durant	
Karl	Lilgert	
Kate	Fish	
Kathy	Copps	
KC	Kachaluba	
Kim	Zang	9

Kristin	Miller	48
Larry	Iverson	
Laura	Yerex	
Les	Wagner	
Leslie	Sattich	
Lillian		
Linda	Gibbs	26
Lorrie	Thompson	39
Lou	Allison	30
Madelaine		
Madoka		
Maggie	Bryan	
Margaret	Logan	
Margo	Elfert	20
Maria	Parks	17
Maria	Manitopyes	
Marie	Meynen	33
Marty	Sutmoller	17
Mary		
Michael	Gabriel	
Mike	Crawford	
Misae	Carlson	
Monika	Terfloth	
Nancy	Fischer	6
Nancy	Latham	13
Nancy	Lagey	
Nancy	Wilde	
Nicole	Aseuge	
Nicou	Revel	19
Nina	Merette	
Norah	Clarke	
Norah	Fish	
Norma+John	Leakey	

Peggy	Carl	
Peter	Kohler	
Raseel		
Rheannon	Brooks	
Richard	Fish	
Rowena	Mitchell	
Sandy	Galletti	6
Sarah	Ridgway	
Sheila	Seideman	16
Sheila	Dobie	48
Sheila	Nelson	
Sheila	Osterhold	
Shelley & Bill	Lobel & Edbrooke	22
Sonja	Suttmoller	
Su-San	Brown	
Sue	Staehli	
Ted	Gibbs	
Ted	Invictus	
Thora	Brooks	
Trish	Sarazin	
Wendy	Borden	29
Wendy	Brooks	34
Wendy	Poole	

List of Quilts Mentioned and Links

Amber's Quilt, 131
Bobby's Quilt, 160
Brandin's Quilt, 71-72
Carol's Challenge Quilt, 149
Carol's Quilt, 103
Cato's Quilt, 67-68
Claire's Quilt, 71, 110, 157
Dodge Cove Counting Quilts, 147
Dolly's Challenge Quilt 2010, 160
Dolly's Quilt, 108, 122, 123-124
Dory's Quilt, 85-86, 160
Elize's Quilt, 65-66, 67
Elron's Quilt, 44-45
Emily's Quilt, 105, 122, 157
Emma's Quilt, 155
Finn's Quilt, 103-105
Fran's Quilt, 137-138
Gabriel's Quilts, 81-82
Galen's Quilt, 41-43, 155
Grant's Quilt, 82-84, 85
Hayden's Quilt, 160
Joline's Quilt, 97
Kai's Quilt, 122, 160
Karen's Challenge Quilt, 148
Kim's Quilt, 99, 100-101
Kristin's Quilt, 110-112, 113-114
Levi's Quilt, 147
Linda's Quilt, 117, 118, 119, 120
Lorrie and Paul's Quilt, 43, 45, 160
Lou's Quilt, 5, 144

Luca's Quilt, 145
Malcolm's Quilts, 150
Marie's Quilt, 67, 122, 156
Maxim's Quilt, 110
Mia's Quilt, 79-80, 110
Morgan's Quilt. 43-44
Moss's Quilt, 148-150, 153
Nicou's Quilt, 115
Norah C's Quilt, 105
Oceane's Quilt, 148
Olivier's Quilt, 109
Rheannon's Quilt, 69
Richard's Quilt, 158
Rowena's Quilt, 105
Rylan's Quilt, 159
Sarah's Challenge Quilt, 154
Siobhan's Quilt, 68-110
Thora's Quilt, 69
Tlell's Quilt, 41-42
Yavonnah's Quilt, 42, 43

Kristin's website and blog: Knotsandstitches.ca

Coastal Quilts Slideshow: Knotsandstitches.ca/slideshow

*Gumboot Girls: Adventure, Love, and Survival on BC's North Coas*t:
Caitlinpress.com/Books/G/Gumboot-Girls

Gumboot Girls (and Guys) Facebook page: facebook.com/GumbootGirls

Gumboot Guys: Nautical Adventures on British Columbia's North Coast:
Caitlinpress.com/Books/G/Gumboot-Girls

Innovative Group Quiltmaking in an Isolated Coastal Community in British Columbia, Canada: Out of the Mainstream (Kristin's 1993 research paper):
kora.quiltindex.org/files/35-90-171/Uncoverings1993-A4.pdf

About the Author

Photo Vivien Kuehl

After her early days as a waitress, Kristin Miller worked as an occupational therapist. After abandoning that career, she was a housemother at a group home for teens, worked on a fish farm, coordinated a mental health activity program, and became a professional quilter. Kristin has created hundreds of art quilts and custom quilts, and has involved others in group-made friendship quilts and protest quilts. She is the author of *The Careless Quilter: Decide-as-You-Sew, Design-as-You-Go Quiltmaking*. She wrote a research paper about the Coastal Quilters for the American Quilt Study Group, and contributed a chapter to *Gumboot Girls: Adventure, Love & Survival on the North Coast of British Columbia*. She lives in Powell River, BC, and enjoys reading, gardening, boating, dogs and red wine.

Please visit Kristin's website, *knotsandstitches.ca* for more colour photos of the quilts, and blog posts about the quilts and life across the harbour and beyond.